HAUNTINGS

OF THE

KENTUCKY STATE
PENITENTIARY

STEVE E. ASHER

To my family

I love you Cheyenne, Alyssa, Cailyn, Makenzie and Ivan.

You make this life have meaning, and Joseph and Kaylee, you give me hope for when I too pass through the veil. I hope to see you both again.

A PERMUTED PRESS BOOK
ISBN: 978-1-61868-691-6
ISBN (eBook): 978-1-61868-692-3
HAUTNINGS OF THE KENTUCKY STATE PENITENTIARY
© 2016 by Steve E. Asher
All Rights Reserved
Cover art by Quincy Alivio

Frontispiece Photography by Steve E. Asher

PERMUTED
PRESS

Permuted Press, LLC
275 Madison Avenue, 14th Floor
New York, NY 10016
permutedpress.com

CONTENTS

INTRODUCTION

You may know the prison as "the Castle on the Cumberland," "Maggie's," "the Pen" or simply "KSP." The Kentucky State Penitentiary has always been an eerie place surrounded by dark rumors. This has been so since its initial construction in the mid-1800s.

The prison is located in sleepy Lyon County Kentucky and is the dark sentinel on the water. The penitentiary is a massive edifice overlooking what had once been the old city of Eddyville. This was a long time ago. The place had been home to many, long-term, local families. The town was later flooded to make the massive waterway that now lies in front of the prison.

The Kentucky State Penitentiary has a long history, and has long been a place of misery and brutal justice.

"Abandon all hope ye who enter here"

This was the inscription at the gates of Hell from Dante's *Inferno,* and this same quotation on a plaque greeted those condemned to serve their time as they entered the gates of the prison. This set the tone for their sentences. There would be no mercy found inside this institutional machine of pain. There would be no attempts at rehabilitation. The prisoner would only encounter a high death toll from disease, poor sanitation, and poor diet, a death toll that was of staggering proportions.

The very design of the prison cast a long, dark shadow that permeated the lives of all those incarcerated there and for well over one hundred years. Italian builders modeled the prison on a medieval castle. Their first look gave pause to even the most hardened criminals who were unlucky enough to be in such a dark place. Those who stood before the penitentiary felt great unease. This was not a place built for reformation or reflection.

The prison, as the name implies, was a tool to press the convicts into a life of punishment and self-reflection. Extreme isolation and grueling labor forged terrible physical and mental consequences. The tactics were to enforce control and to subjugate the inmates. The prison was not just built to house prisoners. The place was also meant to be a warning and example of the penalties one would face for all those who might dare to entertain the thought of a life of crime.

The modern prison is now quite a different institution altogether. The current penitentiary is a place governed by strict laws and oversight. The rights of the inmate get serious consideration before any move-team is assembled or any memorandum is posted for updated changes in policy. The way inmates get housed is different as well.

Kentucky has just one super maximum-security institution, and the Kentucky State Penitentiary is it. The penitentiary has a Death Row section, as well as medium and minimum-security sections. There is a protective custody area, as well. Each section, or class, as they are sometimes referred to, has separate housing assignments.

Stringent rules have always dictated the inner world of the prison. To this day, the place remains isolated. The result is an institution that is a secretive community of harsh control and frequent savagery. Furthermore, this seems partially the result of the fact that the prison is a for-profit institution. The staff is composed of local men and women.

Over the years, things have changed somewhat for the better at the prison. The brutality was far worse in the early years of the place. Those in control at the time would house lifetime killers along with petty criminals, and this made for terrible consequences for those who weren't convicted of the more terrible crimes.

Often, these inmates lived in fear of the more brutal ones, and with good reason, for they were no match for the truly vicious felons incarcerated there. Even children—those compelled by hunger to steal a single loaf of bread—could end up at the penitentiary. Those often fell prey to the more brutal inmates. This arrangement was due to the fact there was little difference between the custody scores of different types of criminals in those days. Custody scores determine the threat level of an inmate.

Therefore, the years of confinement of anyone at the penitentiary were hellish. The lives they lived were full of dread and brutal circumstance behind the coarse limestone walls of the medieval-looking prison. The conditions were so inhuman, that often even a short stay of just six months could be a virtual death sentence.

Symbols of one's potential doom were everywhere in the place. For example, in plain sight in the prison yard stood the imposing edifice of the gallows. These were always open for business, it seemed, and executions were a common thing. In the region of the prison, bootlegging was a crucial means of survival for many of the local inhabitants.

Moreover, many of the poor found a chance to make good money during the period of alcohol Prohibition of the 1920s and early 1930s. Therefore, ending up imprisoned at the penitentiary was always a very real possibility for convicted bootleggers. In fact, the prison was a final destination for many poor locals driven to commit crimes.

However, the penitentiary did help the local economy. Prison work was always a way for people to better themselves, if through less than conventional means. The prison was one of the few places that never closed its doors. The area's young and poor came from surrounding counties with high hopes of employment.

The place existed in a strange sort of symbiosis. Many locals thrived for generations by working there, while other locals ended up incarcerated and dying there. Nepotism ran rampant at the prison. To see third- and fourth-generation correctional officers in the prison's employ wasn't unusual.

Those earliest days were tumultuous. Deaths were all too commonplace at the prison. This was often the result of violent attacks by inmates on each other. The consequences of hard labor and disgusting housing conditions also contributed to the high body count. This deplorable situation created a veritable powder keg.

Many people believe that a haunting can occur where there is great loss of life, especially under tragic or horrible circumstances. It is said these places become the perfect habitats for tortured spirits and ghosts to dwell. A lifetime of savage and deviant behavior does not fade with death, it seems. The evidence I've found suggests such evil forces might even grow when the spirit is free of the body. This power often seems to morph souls into deranged spirits, often of unconscionable rage.

We will take a closer look at why I've come to believe this idea to be true. I will provide evidence. This will not be just anecdotal evidence of others. I've included cases from firsthand experiences that I've endured. Furthermore, I will show that the Kentucky State Penitentiary is a haunted place. The prison is a place where tortured souls and the spirits of the damned still reside. How can I know this firsthand? Because, for a long time, I was a guard at that nightmare prison...

CHAPTER 1

HOW IT ALL BEGAN FOR ME

I always had an interest in the paranormal and the macabre. I would often read alone in my bedroom as a boy. I read about ghost stories including folklore and urban legends. The vivid, rich storytelling with the eerie settings enthralled my young and hungry mind. All of this sparked my love of literature. The books that made me keep the lights on at night were the best. The light burning late at night in my bedroom meant I was reading a great story.

I was always in the George Coon Public Library in downtown Princeton, Kentucky. You would find me in the 133 Section. This was the Esoteric and Paranormal Section and this held spooky tales and supernatural subjects. Witches to extrasensory perception and cryptozoology (the study of mythical creatures) all fascinated me. I think I read every book in that section.

Perhaps these subjects were just pulp reading to some. However, those books were an escape from a rough life at home. Yes, I received some odd looks from my family and friends with my choice of books. Still, I was in heaven when I was reading such topics.

This love of reading such things went a long way in influencing the topics that I would later write about, the subjects that would hold my interest. I had been a musician and a steel worker as well as a disk jockey before eventually becoming a prison guard. I even later added ghost hunter and deputy jailer to my resume. Yet through all these occupations, my interest in the paranormal only grew, and this was for several reasons, as evidenced in the stories below. The following tales are not fiction. They are all things I had experienced firsthand while working ten years in corrections.

Correctional professionals have given other accounts to me in confidence, as well. They, too, are included in this book, although their names have been changed to protect their privacy. This is because most correctional officers and inmates are a tight-lipped lot.

They do not easily admit to experiencing many odd things at work. They only tend to speak on such matters when they are kept up at night with worry and concern. Only under such circumstances, when pushed to such extremes of troubling doubts, will they finally open up to someone.

The thin blue line is a very real thing for me. Therefore, I've taken great care in showing the proper respect to these men and women who serve to protect us, and who have trusted me enough to share their experience. Again, I use initials and false names in this book in order to protect their privacy.

When one lives in a small town, they have to navigate the rigid ideas of what the locals believe to be reality. Religion, family, work, and football make up the substance of life in such places. The subject of ghosts and the supernatural tends to be anathema to such people, who live a practical daily existence, as they see it.

In the one hundred plus years in which the Kentucky State Penitentiary has stood brooding atop a lonely hill, no one has ever come forward with this information. This may be due to religious dogma or just a general disinclination or inability to approach this subject. My hope is, by publishing this book, to remedy the silence with regard to all this. I feel this is a story that needs telling. This experience is one that screams, "Tell them! Tell them all."

This is the only such book ever to document the subject of the paranormal with regard to this prison. I felt compelled to see this book written. I hope you enjoy reading this book as much as I did in writing it.

CHAPTER 2

TWENTY RIVER WALK

The time was early February of 2004. My wife, Cheyenne, and our three baby daughters were living in a small home in the rural Farmersville, Kentucky area. We had relocated there. This is where my forebear, William Ashurst Sr., owned many tracts of land and first established us in the then-growing community. Time moved on. Our family numbers grew and spread throughout the city of Princeton and to the surrounding area, so there were a lot of us by the time we moved.

There was an odd thing. I had grown up here, eagerly exploring all the side streets as a young latchkey kid. Both of my parents had worked to support us seven children. However, I mostly cared for myself. Often I would slip out at night to explore the deserted streets of downtown.

I would gather up some crackers and bologna from our kitchen, and head out, eventually to climb up one of the old buildings in town by means of a rickety fire escape. I would camp out up there and just watch the lights of the city until the first hint of dawn came to the skies. This had been my private spot and my special time. I did nothing wrong, mind you, beyond the possibility of a vagrancy charge. I was perhaps twelve or thirteen and my head was mostly in the clouds at the time, it seemed.

It was a quiet little southern town and I was eager for the day to leave it behind me. I had dreams of becoming a musician, and this particular pond was just too small for my big aspirations. I grew older and I played here and there near town.

Nothing very noteworthy came of it. I was just a young man struggling against the flaccid music scene of the region. I in time met Cheyenne, and then things changed for the better.

A short courtship followed. We started a family. We resettled in Princeton. I needed to find gainful employment. I had a limited range of skills. The ones I could most readily utilize were ones I had gained working for the commonwealth at the Western Kentucky Correctional Complex.

I worked there over three years and found the job tedious and unfulfilling. We moved north for a few years to Illinois. However, we missed the Bluegrass State, so we moved back. I again looked to the State of Kentucky for employment, and obtained a position at the Kentucky State Penitentiary.

I was excited at the chance to go inside the Big House. I knew well the dangers that resided there. Still, the prison also meant a steady paycheck. Moreover, there was my morbid curiosity. I had heard some bizarre stories about the Kentucky State Penitentiary from my father. He had worked there before becoming a police officer. He had always warned me to avoid the place if possible. This just added to the forbidden quality of the setting for me. I was intrigued.

In retrospect, I realize my father's repeated admonishments had been more than just the standard father's concern for his child. There had been a true urgency in his voice whenever he spoke of the prison and why I shouldn't end up there.

The subject seemed actually to weigh on him. I learned the topic of the penitentiary was not something you brought up with my father. Not until much later in his life, did he admit to having had some paranormal experiences while employed there, and this had been the reason for his warning to me. Furthermore, these were stories he had not wanted to talk about, not ever, nor the fact that the shadows that lurk inside the cells, and within the prison in general, eventually became a part of you.

Having this knowledge gave me a deeper wariness for the institution than I already had. In the beginning of my job, part of my work during Officer Common Core In-service Training revolved around the early years there. In the process, I learned more of the violent history of the penitentiary. The place had been an inmate battleground. Much of this was due to the harsh, institutionalized setting of those confined there.

I had been there about three months at the time of my first weird incident. One thing I need to explain before relating this event: going to the prison was, for me, to face a total flip in policy from the Western Kentucky Correctional Complex. W.K.C.C is a minimum-security satellite work farm for the penitentiary.

Most locals called it "the Farm." The complex held inmates inside a dormitory-type of setting with bunks in various sleeping quarters on a large open field. The Farm looked nothing like the noisy, closed-in cells of the penitentiary.

The inmates of my old workplace had come and gone as they pleased (within the fence perimeters). The security was at a minimum at the farm, much more relaxed. The penitentiary was just the opposite. Therefore, my new place of employment was a reality check for me.

My whole mindset had to undergo a massive reset. Compared to "the Farm," the Kentucky State Penitentiary was like going from relative peace of a sunny day to a brutal and oppressive night.

As events unfolded, I had been working one morning in the Number Four Cell House Control Center. The cell house is a massive white-stone building. It was the kind of place people tend to envision when they watch old prison movies. The building had heavy, chain-driven iron gates at the entrance. There were tall, double-tiered cells. Chain-linked fences topped with barbed wire encircled the main living area. The purpose of this fence wasn't just to keep inmates from escaping, but was also in part to prevent "swan dives" by prisoners, who sometimes committed suicide by plummeting several stories down to the unforgiving prison floor. Prisoners often chose this method of death when they had lost all hope and given up.

It was terrible to be a witness to such a death. One could hear their head split open like a ripe watermelon when they crashed into the ground.

The central control post where I was stationed controlled all the electronic locks to the inmate cell gates. Prior to my arrival, and before this arrangement, things before had been much harder. All cells then had to be unlocked by hand with a master key. This, by the way, is the origin of the term, "turnkey."

This had made for hellish emergency let-outs, so the more modern system was much better. The control center's double switchboard could and did control each prisoner's movements in and out of the cell house. This system also controlled the prison yard gate, as well as the gates to the Administration Building.

More security features existed. The prison had cameras to monitor activity up and down the darkened cell walks, as well. There was also outer fencing, because prior to this, with just railings in place, other inmates had tossed men over them to their deaths for squealing to the authorities.

After the change had been implemented, such murders could no longer be committed. On that one day, we had just completed a general let-out. This was for non-Death Row, non-protective custody inmates to go eat. The walk officer busied himself with his usual rounds. He made a lockdown sheet for me to be able to set the control board for the lunch let-out.

The mixture of the mundane side-by-side with a high probability for extreme violence was what made the Kentucky State Penitentiary such a unique place to work, and often a dangerous one. The prison was always a place of fear. The ever-present hand of possible death was felt everywhere. As a result, mortality was always on one's mind.

The house walk officer was making a round when something strange caught my eye on the camera monitors. I leaned in closer toward the small screens. These were just above the illuminated control boards. At first, I thought what I saw was in an inmate passing another inmate some sort of contraband. I started to radio the walk officer to go check this out. However, something caused me to pause.

This was something new to me. Up until this point, I had seen very little that I could call paranormal in nature. Most incidents, I'd previously come across I had just explained away as due to various weather conditions, different tricks of lighting, and such. What followed next was not one of those things. This one transcended the explainable. Moreover, this began my venture into high strangeness, because this was my first experience of The Kentucky State Penitentiary's brand of the occult.

I was looking at an area known as the River Walk, which of course, received the name as this was along the riverside of the building. There was a single row of cells beyond a thin security fence there. This location held a chill year round. The area was even freezing in the mammoth heat of August. Oddly, this had area been the site of several previous paranormal occurrences, or so I had been told.

As I watched, the spectral occurrence began to show itself to me on the small black-and-white screen of the monitor. It was as if there was a faint ripple in the air as the "energy," which is the only way I can describe it, appeared. This phenomenon started slowly. The thing, like a pale streak of light, was barely discernible. Then, whatever it was, it gained strength. I widened my eyes in disbelief as I watched this unfold.

What was I looking at? I wondered. The image did not appear human. Rather, the thing was a dark shape, one the waxed and then waned, before again swelling more strongly into view once more.

I had the distinct impression I was witnessing intelligent movement there. How I could know this I'm not sure, but this was the feeling I getting from it. It was as if some form of a sentient shadow was moving along the far end of the empty walk. Worse, the feeling I had was that the black form somehow knew I was watching it as well, although how this could be, I had no idea.

As I continued watching, the vague form twisted and separated into several smaller dark segments before rejoining. The shade, which was the only way I could think of it, hovered there in the dull, yellow, half-light of the fluorescent overhead lamps that flickered there. I could definitely see the presence of "something." The impression I had was that the spirit, or whatever it was, darted in and out of the cell gate fronts.

"What is this unliving thing up to and what does it want? What the hell?" I half-muttered to myself. I had no idea what I was looking at, or rather, I had an idea, but the implications of it scared me. So I just sat there, stunned.

The shadow then faded from sight, like an ember dying, finally winking out. I turned toward the dull metal stairs, when I heard the walk officer approaching my gate. He carried the lockdown sheet. Reaching the gate, the officer pushed the sheet between the bars toward me. After I had taken it, he made his way to his chair, sat, and then fumbled in one of his coat pockets. I guess he was ready for a smoke after the long walk he had taken.

I was right. He lit up a cigarette and then began updating his logbook.

I saw something on the screen again. There was more movement happening on the lower walk. This is something eldritch and alien beyond anything I had ever witnessed before. This was no mere passing shadow I was witnessing. I was convinced of that. This "presence" was something real. From the shadows appeared a large, bluish-white orb, one nebulous appearing in nature. The sphere drifted forward.

The shadow or apparition appeared to be nearly two feet in diameter. The dark energy appeared animated by some powerful supernatural force. The anomaly moved up and down, drifting and hovering like some kind of weird fog approximately four feet above the concrete floor. There was no audible sound as this took place. No shadow was cast on the floor or anywhere else I could see. The orb gave off an inner illumination whose source I could not explain. This was no trick of light or daydream. This was real.

I stood up and tried to adjust the contrast on the old gray monitor in an attempt to sharpen the image more. Those state monitors were ancient. The brightness of this roiling mass had now become too fiery for the camera to process. The phenomenon kept causing bleached-out flashes to streak across the monitor. I tuned the brightness down and managed a clear image at last. What I saw inside the strange mass was a near perfect image of a human torso with no arms or head.

I felt as if I were witnessing something very old, although why I felt this, I couldn't say. The bizarre form seemed only semi-solid. I experienced fear, and I realized it was the fear of someone looking onto something not of this world. The bright orb pulsed in random-seeming patterns. The flashes illuminated the cell front like a Fourth of July sparkler display. I stood transfixed by all of this.

After a time, this ended. The apparition, of a sudden, darted to the right and then back. The thing rushed toward the camera and then off to the left, finally disappearing off the monitor. The walk went dark once again. I readjusted the monitor to the regular settings, but now there was no trace of anything ever having been there.

I stared, amazed by all this. Then, reality came back with a thump. I jerked back and I fell back into my office chair. I gasped out to myself, "Where the hell did that thing go?" The monitor now still showed nothing more than a deserted prison walk. The cell fronts again appeared cold and dark, just as before all this had begun.

I had to know what I had seen. This was not something I could just let go unanswered. I sat there for several stunned minutes trying to figure out how best to solve this. My mind scrambled to find a reason why and how this had happened. The walk officer rose to get a drink of water from the water cooler. He paused in order to glance to his right.

He studied the shadowy staircase. The metal steps wound down to the narrow Twenty River Walk. The officer began to move toward his desk. I stopped him. However, instead of speaking immediately, I just stood there a moment. I was unsure how to approach the subject.

I did not want to come off sounding like some sort of a crazy person, so I weighed my words with care. In as calm a voice as I could muster, I asked the walk officer to make a quick round down on Twenty River Walk. I figured it was best just to make sure nothing was burning, causing any sort of smoke. It was also a good way to see if anything was out of place.

He squinted at me a moment, studying my face. He must have seen the concern there. Then, the officer obliged my request, without questioning as to why I wanted him to do this. I watched him go up and down the walk. He used his flashlight to make sure all was well. I watched the screen and could see him then moving back up the walk.

He returned and reported there was nothing out of the ordinary. "All cells are empty and all the lights are out," he said. He also reported no coffee pots were on, either. He couldn't find anything that would have produced smoke or vapor.

I let the matter go. The day wore on. On a regular basis, I studied the camera monitor on Twenty River Walk. Nothing more happened. The normal daily routine had returned without any further incidents.

It was about ten minutes until my shift change when the walk officer walked up to my gate. He had worked twenty years as an officer of KSP and so had a lot of experience. He was also as stoic a man as I had ever encountered. He did not seem to be one that entertained any thoughts of ghosts or weird apparitions. This made what he said next even more surprising.

"Okay Asher," he said. "What's going on? You've been like an eagle watching those monitors since this morning. Whatever it is, you seem kind of on edge from it." He gave me a knowing look, as if he already knew why I had been behaving the way I had.

"You would never believe me, even if I told you, sir," I said. I didn't want someone I respected to think less of me. I supposed I could have played the whole thing off in a nonchalant manner, except for how vivid the spectral image had been.

He gave me a sly smile, then replied, "I bet, I just might. Tell me what's going on." I explained what I had experienced in the control room. His reaction to my explanation surprised me.

He said, "Yeah that sounds about right. This place is a spook's wet dream. You can't go a week without something freaky happening. We lose a lot of officers to seeing stuff like that."

This was both a chilling revelation and a relief at the same time. He went on to explain that Twenty River Walk had been, for a very short time, Death Row. Moreover, the walk was across from the cell house showers where many murders and rapes had happened. All of that could have played a huge hand in any supernatural strangeness the place had acquired. "It's like a God damn rogue's gallery in here," the old officer added.

I learned these sorts of apparitions were what passed for normal at the prison. Many things had contributed to life being short for inmates in the early days of the penitentiary. The ventilation on the lower prison walks had not worked well. Many men died from exposure to sewer gas. This was also a very easy way to contract some deadly disease, because dangerous bacteria were rife.

As a result, not just guards, but also many inmates swore they have seen a thing no longer human roaming the walks at night.

The guard confided he had often seen fast slinking shadows there. He had heard disembodied voices in unoccupied cells. The officer had even heard what sounded like leg irons clanking and crying children.

He followed this information up by saying, "You may learn to manage the activity but this will never, ever feel normal. Oh and by the way, welcome to The Kentucky State Penitentiary, kid."

I had worked this post on many occasions. I had worked the walk at Four Cell House several times since that incident. There are quite a few places where the presence of "something" being there is obvious and undeniable at times. I've found cold spots and seen glimpses of things out of the corner of my eye before. However, nothing had compared to the scale of this particular encounter.

People may try to refute this. All I know is that I lived through it. It was real. One may ask me: "Are these phenomena some type of ghosts or spirits? Are they demons, perhaps?" I can't answer that. I don't know with any real certainty just what they are.

Still, I am convinced they exist, even if I don't know what their exact nature is. If these things are able to pass through thick walls of stone or as some light streaming through a windowpane, what keeps them here in our world at all? What tied them to the place of misery and death that was the penitentiary? The only answer I can come up with is just that, somehow, the apparitions are bound to the prison because of so much wretchedness and death having taken place there.

My time at the prison did not leave me unscathed. The unique experience of having been haunted at the Kentucky State Penitentiary has opened my eyes to the fact there are things beyond our world, beyond what we can control. That day changed me. The world beyond this world had opened to me As a result; I awaited the next chance to experience the phenomenon again. It would not be long in coming.

CHAPTER 3

THE BLOODY EARTH KENTUCKY STATE PENITENTIARY

"This place sits on blood as surely as it does on stone and earth." This is how one person described to me the tumultuous history of the Kentucky State Penitentiary. I had not been a member of the special operations team. Yet, I've seen secret places there. I've borne witness to what lies there.

There are few which have ever seen these locations. The special operations teams have full clearance to use all the passages under the prison. Many of these are tunnels opened only in times of riots. Until needed for such a purpose, the dark accesses stay locked.

With a sense of some trepidation and, yes, wonder as well, I would seek them out at times. I've peered into the deep dank passageways that run beneath the prison. I've even touched the original thick wooden doors that at one time hung on the heavy iron hinges in front of the prison.

When I've run my hands over the richly worked wood, my thoughts raced. How many thousands of souls have had their fates sealed behind these doors at one time or another? Such a bizarre piece of art, these doors, left for display at this lost and unforgiving place. The very idea of this was ridiculous to me, macabre.

I've learned firsthand one thing: behind those prison walls lie forsaken spirits, dark souls now twisted and feral. They are the black things. I've seen firsthand how they move as shadow haunting the prison confines, frightening many officers and inmates alike who have to live and work there, even to this day.

Some might question how such a thing can be, can exist, or even be possible at all. Different paranormal investigators explain this in different ways. My approach, based on my experiences as an investigator, is that there is a form of condensed paranormal energy that can occur, one that amplifies the wickedness of people's minds.

To claim the penitentiary was haunted only due to there being criminals within the walls of the impressive keep just does not explain it all for me. Why do I think this? Well, other prisons of equal stature do not have such reputations. What is that old expression one uses in these situations? "Blood will tell?" In this case, this may be literally so.

I believe one does not construct a world of and for murderers, and think it will not then act according to its own unique nature. Some place this happens, while other places, it does not seem to and the reason for this may be there has to be a sort of path for such things to grow, develop and then take place.

Many paranormal investigators believe that the path is already there to begin with, and all the energy then has to do is to follow it into our world. The governor at the time of the completion of the initial build said the following. "The Kentucky State Penitentiary was a disastrous idea and one I regret." He may never have spoken truer words.

The very walls of the prison grew on inmate labor. The stone for them came from large limestone blocks quarried from the local earth. The parcel of land the penitentiary occupies is made up of solid limestone.

How is this important? Well, it is the belief of many paranormal researchers that magnetite plays a huge role in haunting reports. Magnetite can be one of limestone's key components. Magnetite, as many know, has strong electromagnetic properties. For this reason, some investigators of the occult believe limestone can hold onto spirit energy.

Rather like a giant battery or condenser for occult power, such limestone may act not only to record horrendous events, but then replay those terrible scenes at various times, given the right conditions. In the case of the Kentucky State Penitentiary, this would seem to be even truer than might be usual.

Not only does the prison have the perfect physical characteristics to create such a horrendous environment, in everything from the land it sits on, its foundations, and even the very building and walls of the place, but it certain had the needed amounts of human misery having taken place there, as well. In my opinion, never had a truer house of horrors existed in the Bluegrass State, and, worse, it had existed for a long time.

If the paranormal investigators are right, this was more than time enough for all the hate the forced laborers not only to imbue the very makeup of the prison, but for it to grow even fouler, as well. Every single black thought and sadistic dream could well have soaked into the matrix of the structure, like spiritual arsenic into those heavy stone blocks.

One thing seems certain regardless of how it is explained, and that is a dark presence had taken residence at the penitentiary. The very rock that formed the prison's foundations now seemed permeated with evil.

As a further argument for this, many paranormal experts say moving water can intensify this effect of the magnetite in limestone. They argue that with the latent supernatural force, combined with the additional magnetic field produced by moving river water nearby that this helps the dark energy to grow to formidable proportions and power. My belief is that it is a force. This force or influence not only affects the inhabitants of the prison, but moves beyond the borders of the penitentiary property, as well. Sightings of wraith-like phenomenon, of seeing spectral lights moving along or dancing up the outer penitentiary wall, are common.

From out of the misty woods that hide the old, indigent-inmate bone yard, one can occasionally hear screams. This place is known by locals as "Vinegar Hill," and seems to have created a nexus of sorts. This nexus would appear to be a place where the barrier has grown thin between the world of the living and of that of the dead. In this raw spot, extraordinary and terrible things might then happen and in some cases, seem to have done so.

There is one final aspect of this particular prison. How it may act as not only an amplifier, but a conduit for the supernatural, as well. There is the fact of the primitive and unshielded electrical work that still exists in parts of the prison to this day. The electrical usage at the prison is massive. That energy consumed requires huge conduits.

The inmate's exposure to the electromagnetic fields, or "EM" fields, as they are called, is twenty-four hours a day. Such might make impact people's health, both physically, but also mentally and emotionally as well, according to some sources. It's eminently conceivable that those who are already patently mentally disturbed could become even more so, become borderline psychotic due to the strength of such EM fields. When the population happens to be so murderously criminal in nature, then perhaps this is even truer.

Based on my feelings and research on the matter while still working there, I submitted a proposal to the warden. My idea was for him to allow me, on one of my days off, to bring in some devices capable of measuring heightened EM fields. I wanted to try to verify the link to peaks in inmate violence as correlated to their prolonged saturation/exposure to electromagnetic fields.

The warden denied my request. I had seen firsthand the effects deprivation and extended exposure to stress have on the people incarcerated in the penitentiary. The harsh and brutal modes of death there sometimes by a prisoner's own hands can leave one feeling numb inside. I've seen prisoners so twisted from their time in the segregation ward that they do themselves grievous physical harm as a result. I was at the penitentiary for something like four months before I had endured my first real taste of the truly terrible aspects of the place. Things would soon become clear enough to me as to what the lasting effects of that damnable place could be on the human psyche.

I was working an evening shift. I was helping with yard security. The thing about evening shifts is it allowed one to get into and explore otherwise forbidden areas with no trouble. This was because the night shift was much more relaxed in its protocols in some respects. Moreover, there weren't many supervisors around the place.

At one point, I had to go over to Three Cell House. There was an inmate "causing a ruckus," as the captain called it. I was making my way across the top of the yard one mid-July afternoon and it was hot as hell. The sun was setting, yet the temperature remained in the upper nineties.

While headed there, one of the other officers accompanying me said, "Maybe it's a hanging. Let's hope so. They're all useless pieces of crap." This was a standard type of comment of the young, gung-ho types who wanted to be tough guys.

Reaching our destination, I unlocked and then entered the gate of the Three Cell House upper yard. I asked the lieutenant there what was going on. He tried to explain the situation over the bedlam. Because of the noise, I just caught part of what he said, because many of the inmates of the cell house were beating and banging on their cell fronts.

The "gung-ho" guard with me asked, "Am I gonna get to crack some convict heads or what?" The lieutenants, as if one, just turned and stared at him.

Doing the wise thing, it seemed to me, the supervisor sent the "super trooper" back up the hill. He then ushered me inside the doorway. I entered the cell house's main floor. One could feel all the crazy in the air, the tension, in an instant.

However, this time, the feeling was something even beyond that. I had assumed this was more or less the high emotional state. I now think the feeling was the overall spirit of the place. The Kentucky State Penitentiary was buzzing. The cell house was a potent battery for the energies of the dead to feed.

I will refer to any inmates with a false name. There were guards scrambling to the lower cage. "The cage" is the control center for Three Cell House. The cage officer tossed me a pair of purple latex gloves. I looked at her with an inquiring gaze.

"You going onto the walk or what?" she asked. Her gray showed through her bad dye job. The hair, which was up in a bun, had now fallen into errant locks across her face.

I replied in the affirmative. I wanted to know just what I was walking into. I stepped in as I pulled on the powdery latex gloves. The tracked gate slid to and locked.

She yelled out, "No time for all that mess. Just follow the screaming. Stop when you see the blood trail. You'll know you got the right cell." This was, in hindsight, unnecessary. I ran down the walk toward a mass of blue uniforms.

I entered the fray. I saw a wiry African American man. He was on his back and struggling with three correctional officers, even though he lay chained to his concrete and steel bunk in a four-point restraint. This technique of confinement immobilized his arms, as well as his legs. He had obviously been very violent, because everything within his reach was bloody.

The security-grated, florescent light hissed and popped angrily in the corner of the wall of the segregation cell. The stale room held onto an unbearable stench, a combination of coagulated blood and unchecked body odors. The inmate's body jerked and contorted. He was in a last and futile attempt to gain his freedom. His eyes rolled back into his skull like those of a child's broken doll.

The guards came together in a coordinated effort and began unfastening the bedside restraints. First, they worked on his leg cuffs. Those that connected to his legs came first and then again cuffed together. The same procedure followed for the arms. The effort was an orchestrated move, and one these men had tended to many times with many inmates.

Each man then took an arm or leg and lifted him free of the bunk. I could see the bedding was wet with blood and perspiration. They removed the gore-covered and now-cursing convict from his cell. The officers placed him into "the seat." This was the name given to the safety restraint chair, a device used when the officers had to deal with a homicidal or suicidal inmate.

The inmates of The Kentucky State Penitentiary would sit in these seats, often naked, for hours on end if they did not calm down. The chair comes out after the "fight" is already out of the prisoners. Therefore, such a device, in my opinion, is a senseless means of torture. I left the cell with the last of the inmate's bloody personal effects. As I went, I saw him sitting there in the seat, bound and helpless. I found him to be a pitiful creature with haunted eyes. He didn't meet my gaze, but instead just stared at the wall.

I noticed there were streaks of fresh blood on his chest. He also had some running down his legs. Blood seemed to be smeared everywhere, including on us. Everyone wore his blood.

The entire walk of jailed inmates was now livid with rage, as if the convict's madness had been catching and they were now infected, as well. However, this time, the uproar seemed more than a simple blood lust to me.

On a gut level, I felt there was an almost supernatural quality to it. It even appeared as if some strange illness had befallen everyone, even us guards. I felt a primeval emotional response rising full and rich within me, as well. I was sure if I did not leave blood-caked, gray-walled cell soon, that my knees would buckle under me.

The supervisor saw me coming toward him. He called out to me, "Hey! Did you grab any towels?"

I shook my head, and replied, "I'm sorry I didn't. No one said for me to bring any along."

"Screw it," he said. "Then we'll just have to make do with what we've got. The dumb son of a bitch is bleeding out everywhere." He had a look of disgust on his face.

I looked at the cheap industrial paper towels, which had been bunched up in the inmate's lap. They were soaked and shiny from the saturation of fresh blood. The darkness of the blood spread like India ink on fresh parchment. The supervisor waved to the nurse who was up the walk. The other nurse who had been on duty had run ahead to the inmate infirmary. We were to follow her once we could get off the cell walk.

The cell house supervisor then told me to take over on the mini DVD camera. This was used to record and document such volatile situations as these, as a way to protect the prison from allegations of wrongdoing. These kinds of incidents often ended by becoming lawsuits. Sometimes, the inmates won. Often, and thanks to the camera recordings, they did not.

As I steadied the camera in my hands, we left the walk. The gate clanged shut behind me with a reverberating sound. I glanced back over my shoulder. I could have sworn I had seen movement from inside the now-empty cell. This was brief and faint movement. Something one might glimpse from the corner of their eye. Barely perceptible, yet the oddity was definitely there.

Before I could voice say anything, the lower cage officer flipped the knob that closed the battered cell front gate. This blocked my ability to see anything further, regardless of whether anything had continued to manifest in there.

I shifted my focus elsewhere because I felt uncomfortable. The inmates on the walk increased their uproar. The closing of the section gate seemed to incense them. The damn cell house now was alive and screaming. Every inmate had gone into a frenzy. I knew the mood of the inmates was now out of control, ungovernable. I wanted none of this. None of us did. We hastened out of the maddened cell house and moved toward the prison infirmary.

Our journey paralleled the inside fences, which lay between Three and Six Cell Houses. I could still hear the screams from behind me as we continued toward the infirmary. The wounded inmate had at last fallen silent. The wheels of the chair crunched through the walkway's loose gravel, as we sped him down to the infirmary. His blood-soaked towel fell onto the ground. I then saw the yawning open cut below his stomach.

This half-crazed prisoner had all but sawed through his penis. The skin around the wound had a grayish, dead-looking cast. When I had asked how this had happened they informed me his mail had a staple left in it. He then worked it into a sharpened edge and tried to slice off his penis.

"Are staples that sharp?" I asked the officer closest to me.

"Not at all. That crazy jerk must have been working at it for hours in there."

What kind of self-hate mixed with a fanatical conviction would you need to do that? I thought to myself.

"He must be crazy. Who the hell does that to themselves?" the front officer asked.

Once we had gained admittance to the infirmary, the convict was transferred to a hospital gurney. Some officers waited at the front desk. Others, their clothing splattered with blood, went to the bathroom to clean up. AIDS, along with hepatitis and a myriad of other blood-borne pathogens, grew in great abundance in what passed as the Kentucky State Penitentiary Petri dish, none of which the prison staff wanted to bring home to their families.

I stood guard as the nurses hurried about the place. They went to the medication storage room in the doctor's office for pain medication. This left me alone with the inmate. We waited in silence. He lay on the gurney under the examination light and rocked his head from side to side. The smell of drying stale sweat and blood again gave me pause.

Without thinking, the question rolled off my lips. "Why did you do this? What would make you want to cut on and mutilate yourself like that?"

He replied, "I ain't crazy. I know they say I am, but they're wrong. There's so much hate here. Something is evil."

He again started struggling against the handcuffs and thrashing about. The nurses returned with a syringe. After a moment of searching to find the vein, one of them stuck the needle in him.

Another brief minute of struggle and his muscles relaxed. His body again went slack upon the gurney. The nursing staff then began the process of trying to reattach the partially severed organ. After the first slice into the inmate's flesh with the scalpel happened, I turned my face away.

The procedure was completed. The inmate stayed confined in the hospital for observation. The wound he inflicted on himself needed constant attention by medical staff.

I happened to be relieving the hospital officer a day or so later, when I noticed the inmate was still there. He was in the sterile hospital wing. I found him in a small, well-lit room. He wore a thin medical gown and stood at the wired glass wall. He stared out the glass with a vacant stare. I asked him the same question again.

His eyes never blinked once. He gave me an "I don't know" sort of shrug. He sat on the edge of the thin metal bed. I then pressed him to answer. I tried to do it in a way so as not to spark another violent reaction from him.

"Officer, may I ask if you're a religious man?" he asked.

I told him, if he meant did I believe in little naked angels who played harps all day sitting around on clouds and shooting arrows at the hearts of lovers then no, I was not.

He attempted at a weak, smile. The medication still maintained its tranquilizing hold upon him. "No, sir. I mean like what happens after you die. Like what about spirits?" He asked this in a slight, medication-induced slur.

I told him, "Well that's a subjective thing. I would agree this is not all there is." He broke his blank stare and turned to face me through the glass.

I moved in closer. I was now almost right at the security window. I stood close enough for my breath to make small condensation spots. I knew if I did not ask him the next question, it was going to drive me crazy.

"I know about that thing inside of the cell. I saw whatever was in there. There was a strange shadow blocking the cell light that caught my eye. Whatever the dark thing is, it appeared evil to me. I cannot imagine being locked up with that day and night." I added, admitting this last to him.

His look was one of confirmation of what I'd said. Then there was a profound change in his body language and a look of dread came over his features. I could see he was thinking this all over. He seemed lost in thought for a moment, then seemed to become aware of me again. "The devil will not leave me alone," he said. "At least, not until I give it what it wants."

This made me consider what he had done to his body. "Are you talking about the cutting?" I asked. He nodded and then went back to his far-off stare.

Now, I could conceivably write this off to a mental condition of his. I am aware such sightings of paranormal figures can result from schizophrenia. However, I intrinsically felt this was something supernatural in nature. My opinion as a paranormal researcher was that this inmate was really suffering from some sort of paranormal presence at the penitentiary.

I knew firsthand that the effects of the prison are insidious and cumulative. Even after my time at the prison had passed, I still could see or hear things. I wasn't alone in this.

On occasion, I would run into former KSP inmates. These men had served their time. Now free, they had restarted their lives on the outside. Given the right circumstances, I would sometimes speak to them about the activity within the "Castle." They often would agree to the idea of a strong paranormal presence resonating throughout the place. They had all had some sort of encounters. Apparently, no one leaves unscarred from the prison, whether guards or prisoners.

Several former inmates I spoke to also stated they felt a sinister power at KSP that it had felt like some blackening tumor growing on their souls. Either one got out of there or one could well go insane.

I should mention here that correctional officers have a higher than average divorce and substance-abuse rate per capita. Moreover, officers destroy themselves at a thirty-nine percent higher percentage than most of America's population. The method may be through alcohol, drugs, or at the point of a gun barrel. The end is always the same. Dead is dead. The effect of the paranormal on those in touch with the prison is also destructive.

With time and distance, I can stand back now and see the full effect of the prison on people, both inmates and officers. The penitentiary's spiritual oppression drove people into such despair. Having "made it out" I now see a correlation between the paranormal and the deterioration of the human spirit inside a prison.

Talking with these former inmates and officers who worked at the prison proved this to me. So engrossed did I become by this phenomenon, that there was a period when I would spend my time away from work doing paranormal investigation with others to investigate all of this.

They were a small group and made up of friends. Many were also correctional officers employed at the Kentucky State Penitentiary. We had done cases in everything from paranormal activity in homes to defunct mental facilities. The fact all had received training in how to conduct a proper investigation and preserve a crime scene made them ideal for this sort of task. I made sure to try to take every precaution I knew of to get untainted results. The team shared the same views. What drove us to do these sorts of investigations? We all felt the paranormal was real. We wanted to find answers. We had to know.

CHAPTER 4

" BOBBY RAY "

Now, I wish to discuss a friend. I will refer to him as Bobby Ray, an alias in order to protect everyone's privacy. I remember when this kid first came up to the prison. He had come to interview for a correctional officer position. I had been at the penitentiary for at least five years already when I first laid eyes upon him. He was a small person. The boy looked like he was twelve. He sported both a faded pink scar across his throat as well as a distinctive raspy voice, due to multiple throat surgeries.

I was working on the front gate then, and I heard older officers taking bets on how fast he would wash out. Most guards held that Vietnam veteran mentality of, "In six months tell me your name, but until then, piss off." This was because turnover was massive due to the potential dangers and working conditions. Making a friend with every new face was tiring and often disappointing. They would often leave. For this reason, most guards felt it was better to hold back and let things play out a little.

His interview came and went much like that of the other thirty potential new hires. I would not see him again for another couple of weeks. When I did, I was working the yard that morning. I was overseeing security of the inmate medical sign-up line. Part of this duty meant having grown men stick their tongues out at you after receiving their medications. This was to verify they had swallowed the stuff.

I was leaning against the concrete half-wall. This boundary ran parallel to the nurse's station, when I heard someone shout out behind me.

"Hello there Mr. Asher, guess who, buddy?" I knew in an instant that it was Bobby. That voice was not an easy one to disguise. I acted surprised all the same. It was good to have an officer like Bobby Ray that I could mentor. The boy might not have had much size to him, but he did have a ton of heart. Think of a little mutt dog that does not back down. Put that in the body of a simple country boy and you have a good description of his personality.

We became inseparable. Some of the older guards at times referred to him as my "mini me." One day, our conversations turned to ghosts and such spooky things. He had admitted to me that he wanted to go "ghost hunting."

I stressed to Bobby Ray the importance of protecting one's self when dealing with spirits. I gave him a crash course in the basics of doing proper paranormal investigations. He was in committed from that point on. The next few years, we, along with the rest of the team, did investigations as our time permitted.

Both he and I were soon working the "midnight shift" I was doing wall stands at the prison by then. A wall stand is a tower along the top of the outer institution's wall, one where an officer watches the prison yard and looks out for attempted escapes. Bobby Ray was working in Five Cell House as a floor officer by then.

Bobby Ray had become a good investigator at this point, as well. He was ceaseless in his drive and had a willingness to do anything for our paranormal group. He was involved with my proposal to investigate Three Cell House's death walk that had I submitted to the warden. Bobby Ray had taken it upon himself to do whatever he could on the job to establish some kind of spirit communication by means of simple paranormal investigation.

For example, he would set several small objects, such as coins or a pencil, in the outer hallway as he made his rounds. Later he would note if there had been any change in their location, direction, or temperature. Some paranormal investigators believe spirits can affect small objects.

He spoke of sometimes hearing a low murmur on his rounds. He said it was not distinct enough to understand very well. He wished he had a voice recorder on him. The machine could have saved the sounds as evidence.

This was about the time when things began to change in a most dire way for little Bobby Ray. He had seen a few strange things working at the prison. Hell, how could one not in that place? We all did. However, he did not scare easily. Still, he did become more and more isolated as time went on.

I knew he had become a new dad with new dad responsibilities. Yet, this went well beyond that sort of behavioral change. Something more was going on with him. To me, he had acquired a sort of haunted aspect.

Bobby Ray had seen eerie shadows moving and felt presences in Five Cell House. The constant exposure to a continuing onslaught of psychic phenomena can wear down even the strongest individual. This seemed the case with Bobby Ray. He became more introspective, more remote. Our conversations with each other became shorter and less frequent. Bobby Ray told me one night that things were getting strange.

He had told me how he kept feeling like something was watching him. Something other than the convicts made him nervous. Bobby Ray was of the Catholic faith, to the point of even giving me a blessed crucifix. I thought on this and suggested prayer or even maybe talking to someone in the clergy. Most of my faith in organized religion by this time had all but dissipated. I was a victim of seeing too many things too often that seemed to defy conventional religious teachings.

Still, I gave Bobby Ray what counsel I could in this regard, but already having five children in tow myself, I knew there was no easy path to coping with the added stress he was experiencing. I felt I could not offer much help beyond having a sympathetic ear.

About a week had passed when Bobby Ray came into officer roll call in the Main Administration Building one day. He walked into the large break room. He saw me sitting at a table adjacent to the large cathedral windows with their heavy iron bars. He placed his blue cooler on the tabletop and then sat across from me. He looked like he had not slept at all that day. His eyes were rimmed red and he looked as if he had lost some weight. In short, he looked like hell.

One of the many mouth-breather types that can gravitate to this kind of work yelled out: "Hey! Bobby Gay! You look almost as bad as you smell!" A gale of laughter broke out in what I thought of as the lower I.Q section of the room. Bobby Ray never even raised his head. He just lifted his energy drink to his mouth and drank deeply from it. I had never seen the man this despondent before.

I leaned in close across the table then, and whispered, "Okay, brother, what the hell is up? This isn't normal."

He responded in that faint and creaky voice that whatever had been droning in his ear at work had now started following him home. The sounds first stayed with him to the front gate. Then they spread to the parking lot. Eventually, the noises stayed with him halfway home on another night. Then, the last night, the sounds had followed him all the way home. This had taken all week to come about. Yet, he had not told me a word about it to me until now.

I advised him to back away from paranormal investigations. I felt he was becoming obsessed. I counseled him to take a break, and so try to refocus.

He snapped back, "Do you think I haven't tried that?" The strain was now even more evident in his face. He added, "It's making me feel crazy, as if I'll never be free of my situation."

Some paranormal researchers believe that oppression by spirits is a very real phenomenon. They say obsession begins benignly enough with the mere feeling of a presence. This feeling can then manifest with such things as seeing shadows and experiencing poltergeist activity, as well. Over a matter of time, this, in turn, can build to full-on possession in some extreme cases. Often, some form of shaman, priest, or other holy man or woman then deals with the situation at this point.

Another friend and I tried to help ease his mind that night, so Bobby Ray wouldn't feel so alone in his situation. Once we all got to our respective posts, we both tried to keep him on the phone. We were cracking jokes and even talking about his truck. Once the kitchen workers started their day-by-day chores in the kitchen at around 4:00 a.m., everyone had to get busy, so we did not speak to each other much more that night. The next few nights were repeats of trying to keep his spirits up, but the last night he said he was sick with something and was not up to talking.

We both were relieved at out posts about the same time. I hurried to catch up with him as he exited Five Cell House and headed toward the yard door. We talked about maybe getting together soon, perhaps for a family barbeque. We both walked down the front steps of the prison together, separated by just a few steps distance from one another. He looked back at me and began to say something.

As he did this, the same idiot as before yelled, "Screw you, Bobby Gay!" That jerk always had it out for Bobby Ray. I never knew why, but he did pick on him a lot. Bobby just turned away, wearing the same look of defeat, and walked on.

Later at home, I received a phone call. I had been asleep and my wife, Cheyenne, awakened me.

Handing me the phone, she said, "Something is off. Something feels wrong." She always had "feelings" about things. I often supposed it might have something to do with her Native American blood. I think she may have read something in the caller's voice, as well.

It was Jimmy. He was an older correctional officer I knew from the prison. He, like me, had been looking after Bobby Ray during the past week.

He said, "Hey Asher, I'm not sure how to really say this, so I'll just say it." I managed to get out a sleepy, "Yeah, man. What is it?" Jimmy paused, then said, "Well, after we all left today from the prison, something happened. Something real bad went down."

"What?" I asked, still only half-awake. The fog in my head still held sway, as I struggled to focus on the distant-sounding voice in my ear.

"It's Bobby Ray. He's dead, Steve." His voice sounded a lot clearer now, too clear, and suddenly too loud.

My stomach gave a lurch. I felt sick. I sat up in bed. I was wide-awake now. "Jimmy, that's one hell of a bad joke," I said, all the while hoping it was just a joke.

Jimmy explained he had received a distress call over his volunteer firefighter radio and that no, he wasn't joking.

I will not recount the gory details of Bobby Ray's death. He was a dear friend and my ward, of sorts. He was not mere story fodder, not to me. Suffice it to say, my friend went home in silence. He then retrieved the shotgun from a corner of his trailer's small living room. He then went to his bedroom and sat down on his bed with the gun in hand. Bobby Ray then ended his pain the only way he felt he could. In an instant, he was gone. I only hope he found the peace in death that he had sought in life.

That jarring event also sounded the death knell for my time with the Kentucky State Penitentiary. I had seen hundreds of people come to work at the prison. I've trained many of them and cared for only a few like a brother. Bobby Ray was one of the best. My disdain for the place and correctional work in general, grew deeper inside my heart. This happened day by day and from week to week, as a gradual, corrosive thing. I finally took my leave from security work altogether.

I would not let the ghosts that had haunted Bobby Ray's last days, and that had dogged his final steps, become mine. He had become my Jacob Marley, that ghost of *The Christmas Carol* fame. It was my warning and wake-up call to get out while I could.

Leaving the prison, I then soon lost touch with many of the correctional officers I had once worked with side-by-side. This was in some part intentional. I wanted a clean break from the prison. I needed a chance to exorcise those demons, both human and paranormal, from me.

I've to say that telling this story has been a cathartic purge for me of sorts, even beyond the ghostly element of it. I feel that boy's death was a true-life cause-and-effect of the oppressive dark energies trapped within the aged and crumbling stone fences of that monstrous prison. Moreover, I believe I've looked hard and long into the belly of the beast and it was a terrifying sight, one I barely escaped, I feel. The penitentiary was, I believe in a very real sense, the literal gates to a hell of some type.

The truth is the prison is as full of tormented souls as any mythical place of eternal suffering ever written about. The Kentucky State Penitentiary remains a place of shades and disembodied cries for help. Many lives are short there. Deaths are common, The body count keeps climbing.

CHAPTER 5

FOUR WALL STAND

Think about what one might witness if one could float high above the landscape of the Kentucky State Penitentiary, if one could see beyond all of the normal let-outs, and the inmate workers going to their various work assignments. I don't just mean the milling about of those burning away the hours of their institutionalized lives so hopelessly in such terrible conditions. I am speaking of the sometimes horrific carnage that has taken place there, as well.

Another event occurred at the backside of the handball court in the exercise yard. Inmates use this area to let off steam through recreation. Overlooking this handball court and the inmate exercise track, is Four Wall Stand Tower. This wall stand is the perfect spot to stop a riot in the making on the low side of the penitentiary because of its commanding view. Little is hidden from the vantage point of the tower.

This almost twelve-foot square wall tower has large glass panels on all sides. These windows allow for a three hundred and sixty-degree view of the prison yard below from its 45-foot high position on the prison wall. The tower comes equipped with a Mini-14 sniper rifle, a service revolver, as well as a sawed-off riot shotgun. The officer that works there maintains ammunition rounds capable of holding off a sizable siege, if necessary.

Any officer posted in Four-Wall Stand knows if an inmate tries to escape over the wall, then he must carry out the most lethal of measures to stop the convict. This means even killing the inmate, if necessary. This knowledge is enough in itself to play darkly on one's mind while on duty there, and as the night drags on, this feeling only worsens.

Again, the view from the tower is a commanding one. The guard post has a clear vantage point of both the back of the yard office and most of the cell houses. One also can see all of the prison industries. However, over time, the Four Wall Stand post went from a full twenty-four hour shift down to opening at 2:00 a.m., and then until just after final lockup on evening shift.

It could be a lonesome post. Still, in a way, I found that I rather enjoyed the duty. If we had the benefit of a normal F.M. radio on the post, it would have been perfect. I had about five years of working at the penitentiary by then and had transferred to morning shift to better help my family out with daytime appointments.

Being a night owl by nature, this transfer also worked better for me in that regard. In short, working at Four Wall Stand was near perfect for me. There is a locked metal door at the base of the stand, and several reinforced fences surround that base, so it well protected.

The interior of the wall stand boasted a sixty-step, metal set of stairs going nearly straight up. One could see them rise higher into the darkened shaft toward the small post far above. If one were to fall, this would be a terrible fate indeed. I had heard talk of an officer that had fallen. He had died due to the injuries he had received from the fall. However, I was never able to prove or disprove this story, and it might have been nothing more than a cautionary tale, or a sort of prison urban myth for all I knew.

However, this story was often in my mind whenever I would had to work that post, so if it was just a cautionary tale, it worked. The fireman-style steps would echo loudly as one climbed them. The threshold at the top of those stairs had a sheet-metal landing. They would make a loud pop as one entered the small observation post at the top. This was due to any weight being placed on them.

After the prison yard closes to inmate movement on evening shift, the tower is a rather uneventful post to work. That is one reason for the shortening of the shifts there. Being uneventful for the most part, it was on to save the commonwealth money. The Kentucky State Penitentiary was always looking to cut corners anywhere it could. Unfortunately, this often happens by cutting security measures.

"Do more with less." Those who controlled the prison budget lived by this mantra. As one would expect, this system for cutting costs had come back to bite them on occasion.

One night on morning shift, I walked up the front steps of the prison. It was a cool fall evening, crisp. I stood at the front gate waiting to be scanned for admittance. Scanning was a time-consuming process. One has to present their identification card. They then would have their food bag searched for contraband. The bag went through an x-ray machine.

I always even had to go through a metal detector to make sure I had not attempted to sneak in a gun inside of the prison. I never missed the irony of being a prison guard who might have to shoot prisoners, and yet at the same time was checked for firearms upon entering the premises.

Still, we all knew the front gate was how most weapons made their way inside the penitentiary. Furthermore, it was staff, who more often than not, smuggled such items. In other words, nobody could really trust anyone else, not even among the staff. This situation made a friendless and hostile place to work for the most part, with few exceptions, such as Bobby Ray. Therefore, the inmates and the guards were not really so different in some respects. They both were prisoners of sorts of the dark machinery of the Kentucky State Penitentiary.

The time was ten minutes before two in the morning when I made my long trek across the top of the hill toward my post. My gear slung over my shoulder felt like it weighed a ton as I slogged along. I moved through the series of locked iron gates one by one, as I was allowed admittance. The closing of them shook the floor beneath me, even as the heavy leaded sound of them locking once more reached my ears with a sense of clanging finality.

I walked past Four Cell House. I then turned up the steep steps toward the Four Cell House yard gate. Everything seemed uphill for some reason. One always seemed to be climbing rather than descending.

As if the ascent wasn't bad enough, those damnable steps were fearsome in their own right. A slip and then a resulting shattered skull was by no means out of the realm of possibility. Therefore, I approached the stairs with the respect and attention they demanded. I used the radio to signal Ten Wall Stand to let me through the gate. I started out across the barren hilltop.

The first think one notices on such a walk is how cool the night air is atop the hill. This is due to the breeze that blows in from across the nearby lake and then on into the yard. I drew my coat collar up around my neck to try to avoid the cold wind that whistled past me. For warmth, I pushed my hands deep into my coat pockets.

I looked around at the covered picnic area next to the inmate phones as I passed them. A single receiver hung off its cradle and swayed like a pendulum in the breeze. This gave me the feeling I was in the scene of some kind of movie about a dystopian future. You know the type I mean, when one man remains in a vast and empty ruin of a world, and he's just trying to survive.

I crossed over the dull grey sidewalk leading under the shadow of Ten Wall Stand. I could hear the razor wire slapping in the wind against the top of the protective fencing. I saw a small wastebasket-sized trash liner trapped in the security wire. I watched the bag as it whipped about in the gale. I saw the outline of the officer up above me. He stood watching me approach from inside the observation post.

I nodded and gave him a short wave as I hurried onward. Winter was not far off. Already, the prison cats stayed inside or under something to avoid the gale. I moved toward the yard office and then down the stairs leading to the inmate-walking track near the handball court.

This area always gave me the creeps, and not without good reason. The handball court was a site of many stabbings. As I moved on, shadows leapt about, as if playing with each other on the asphalt-walking track. My nightly journey was a cold and somber thing, one I always had to steel myself for.

I met a yard officer who then let me into Four Wall Stand. I needed to count all of my gear and weapons. One has to account for every round of ammunition. I loaded my weapons and looked over the logbook. I watched the video monitors.

We had a telephone and it was more than a way to keep in contact on morning shift. The thing helped us stay awake. As usual, I had been on the phone with another officer this night. He was in another nearby wall stand. My window was open. The cool night air helped me to keep awake.

I studied the cell house roofs for any movement. I saw little beyond a few birds fluttering about the Gothic peaks. I could also hear hungry bats circling the strong overhead lights. They swooped and dove, looking for a nice meal of moths to devour. There were the other sounds of the night. A barge coming through the dark waters in front of the penitentiary blew its lonesome horn.

Night at the penitentiary could fool you. The calm beauty displayed there at times is false. The prison could be, and often was, the site of a violence that could erupt in mere seconds. People like to romanticize the prison, its history, and architecture. In reality, there is nothing romantic about the prison at all.

It was then I heard the bottom door of the wall stand start rattling. The sound was as if a key was going into the lock and being turned. To hear this sort of thing wasn't unusual. The sergeant working yard security might make a surprise wall stand inspection at any time. I ended my phone conversation, assuming this was the cause of the noise I had heard—another inspection. I looked out the window scanning the track field and shadowy ball court below.

I then looked across at the darkened gates leading down to the wall stand. I could not see anyone there. I reasoned the supervisor must have already slipped inside the door and was now at the base of the stairs. I moved toward the narrow opening of the stairwell. I glanced down the steps. I couldn't make out anything moving there. There was no one.

This was all a bit odd, I felt, and yet nothing appeared amiss. I tried to dismiss the sound I'd heard as being only the wind, although there was no longer any breeze. I busied myself with wiping off the counters as well as cleaning the windows. These activities kept my post in good shape, as well as helping me to keep awake and alert.

The night wore on. The time neared 3:30 a.m. I was startled when I again heard a series of noises at the wall stand door. This time, it sounded as if someone was swinging the heavy iron door open. I heard someone moving up the stairs. A steady thudding sort of boom followed, as if someone tread on the stairs.

I was sure this had to be the yard sergeant this time. I put down the spray bottle and cleaning cloth, and again stood ready at the top of the darkened stairs. The sound ceased. I looked to see if there was just me inside of the wall stand. I made certain there was nobody there.

Still, I was perturbed. There was no danger of me getting sleepy now. I became hyper-vigilant in my search for some kind of explanation for the phantom sounds. There had to be a rational explanation, I felt sure. I looked out of the sliding glass windows, studied the structures that were within earshot of where I was, thinking the noises might have somehow come there. Seeing nothing to cause such noises, I then looked around for something that might have come loose somewhere. Maybe, it had caused the sounds I'd heard.

I saw nothing that could have caused such noises. There was simply no reason for the sounds I'd heard. However, if any such noises came again, I planned to be ready the next time.

In the meantime, I tried to relax, endeavored to take my mind off what had happened. I ate the lunch I had packed, and afterwards washed it all down with some strong black coffee. I've got to admit, that at this point, I just wanted out of there. I am not ashamed to say I was more than ready to be relieved at 7:00 a.m. I was in no mood for the apparent game this "thing," whatever it was, was playing.

I had a weapon prepared if something or somebody did try to break into the wall stand. I was determined they would be bullet-ridden and fast. I was not trigger-happy, mind you, but I had no plans on being stabbed to death or being tossed out a window by some convict, either.

I called around to the other wall stands, figuring that someone might have been clowning around. This sort of thing happens on morning shift a lot. The sheer monotony makes people find their own entertainment and this usually takes the form of practical jokes.

All wall stands reported to me there was no one was out in the yard. By now, the time was nearly 5:00 a.m. Things seemed normal enough by this point. All my chores were completed. All was ready for the next shift. I had been updating my logbook now that things had returned to normal. All I had to do was wait to leave.

Then, I again heard the eerie sounds of someone slowly moving up the stairway. Footsteps again treaded upon the stairs, followed by low guttural moans, as well as breathy gurgling. I had been watching the door, but now moved to close the window, feeling I'd be more secure that way. I also called and then talked to another wall stand officer over the phone. I hoped what I was hearing was in reality nothing more than my imagination going wild and thought that by busying myself, I might dispel the strange sounds coming toward me.

The air temperature inside the wall stand suddenly plunged several degrees. Not only was the window closed, but I also had the heat on now, so this should not have been happening. Vainly, my hope was this activity would abate again as before, that it would just go away. I then heard not just the sound of someone climbing the stairs, but something more menacing. The noises continued. Then there was a pause, and the metal landing made a series of "pops," as if someone had made it up to the observation level. Something was out there, less than four feet from me, and in the darkness.

In one swift motion, I dropped the phone and shot up from my seat in a panic. I spun around while drawing my revolver from my side holster at the same time. I scanned the room for signs of life. As my heart leapt in my chest, I leveled my weapon at the last place left to hide there. I aimed my weapon right into the black opening of the stairwell.

After what felt like an endless couple of seconds, I began a slow advance toward that well of darkness. The inexplicable chill still held the room in a deep freeze. Shakily, I shone the flashlight's wobbling beam down into the inky blackness. The flashlight seemed almost dead, so I couldn't see past the first twenty feet or so into the stairwell.

Paranormal experts will tell you the dead are notorious for affecting things around the area of haunting, especially electronic or standard electric devices. The sudden drop in temperature, known as a cold spot, is a common occurrence in ghostly activity. Spirits often seem to draw energy from such things as flashlight batteries. Therefore, all of these events can be signs of a possible haunting.

In any case, this was too much for me after not finding anything yet again. I had had enough of this mental torture. I pulled the hammer back on my service revolver then pointed the nose of my gun down into the cold black opening of the stairwell.

I barked, "OK, you've got my full attention. I got a job to do. So go make rounds elsewhere. I don't have time for your games. " My voice boomed off the gray concrete walls, but there was no answer.

After this, the chill swiftly dissipated and the sounds abruptly ceased. The drained Maglite's beam sprang back to full life. The now radiant light burnt at full tilt. I then remembered I still had my friend on the line. I bent down and picked up the dangling receiver.

Feeling a bit embarrassed, I said, "Man, I must be going nuts. This place has me hearing things."

I was sure he would rail me for barking at an empty room at the top of my voice.

"Well," he said, "if you are crazy, then I am too, boy! I heard that metal popping over the phone. That about knocked me out of my chair."

We talked, as I we both tried to make sense of what we felt certain we had heard. However, I never came to any real conclusions about it all. I even asked myself, "Could this have been the spirit of an officer making a round?" I tended to think so. Some define themselves by the work they do. This is not surprising that some spirits do not want to let go of their previous positions. Perhaps, some guard had worked here once and might have died here.

The years passed. I would have younger officers come and confide to me that they, too, had similar experiences in Four Wall Stand. Most officers hated working that particular post for that reason. They soon learned, though, that very few places did not have some sort of paranormal activity associated with them at The Kentucky State Penitentiary.

CHAPTER 6

BUMPS IN THE NIGHT

We have all caught glimpses of things out of the corner of our eyes, fleeting movements, shifting shadows, that sort of thing. And sometimes, those things can feel sinister, make your hair stand on end. Now, take that experience and place it inside a maximum-security prison. Then just for good measure, have it take place on the midnight shift. This will give you some idea of just how creepy such an event can be.

One night, I was the second-floor walk officer in Five Cell House. By this time, I was looked at as an old timer, having been there ten years. Attrition of workers at the prison was high, so many of the old timers had retired. This left those, like me, with ten years of experience, being the senior officers.

I didn't mind this assignment much. This post was a decent post overall. I had worked this floor for about a year when something occurred. The cell house is located above the inmate kitchen. The kitchen is so old, one can still make out the faded words "black only" painted above the back kitchen doors from the days of segregation. The whites and blacks having to eat separately had been strictly enforced at one time. Those were from the years shortly after the Civil War. Sadly, there were still ghosts of those old racial divisions when I worked there. They exist, but just are not publicly stated.

Inmates still eat in groups more often composed of their race. Moreover, racially motivated fights still happen and often. An inmate talking to another inmate of a different race is considered a serious offense that can lead to punishment from the stronger inmates, those self-appointed guardians of their kind. In addition, I've heard more than my share of racist jokes. Those seem to pass for high comedy at KSP, which gives one an idea of the attitude of those incarcerated there, as well as of many of the prison's employees.

Second floor was general population housing made up of the so-called Alpha and Bravo walk, then the Charlie and Delta walk, and last of all, Echo walk. All had shower stalls located at one end of each walk. These showers were, as a rule, reserved for janitors or painters. The rest had to use the shower house in the yard, unless they had a doctor's note excusing them from this.

Second floor had long been notorious for being roasting hot during the summer, and then freezing throughout the winter. The floor's heat and air conditioning never worked as it should. This had led to a fair amount of fights due to frayed and short tempers. There was always some sort of drama going on, on that floor.

The time was just after 4:00 a.m. and I had just released the kitchen workers to the yard sergeant. He then escorted them to their jobs. The "let-out" went on without incident. The still, half-sleepy men piled into the stairwell. This staircase led to the bottom door of Five Cell House. This door locks everyone inside the cell house at night. Once all the men were off my floor, I secured the wall gate at the front of my post, just as I was supposed to do.

I was doing a lock-down sheet for the house tower officer to be able to set the control room boards for the next let-out. One can set their watch by the let-outs every day. The repetition of this could be both maddening and comforting to the inmates and guards alike. Days could run together, seemingly endlessly, monotonously. The term, "hard time" did not come from a prison stay with hard labor involved. Hard time referred to the fact that time seemed to crawl at a snail's pace.

There is one thing that had always struck me as odd. This was the showers on Charlie and Delta walk. The shower stall was a seven-by-twelve-foot tiled room. There was a small covered light in the ceiling. Even so, the stall always seemed to appear gloomy. Still, there was nothing about the room to warrant the title of being anything but ordinary.

Whenever I would make rounds on that walk, I gave it a wide berth. This was regardless if it were daytime or night. I was not able to explain exactly why I did this, other than it was just a negative sort of feeling. I just sensed there was something "off" about the area, is the only way I can think to explain my feelings with regard to the room. There was something non-tactile about it all. I can only say my feeling was a gut reaction, a sense that bordered on the primitive and the instinctive. The saying, trust your gut. You can count on this response as a tool. Your gut will keep you alive, was very real for me, because it worked.

Thus it was that I was making a round on Charlie and Delta walk, something gave me pause. I could have sworn I had heard a muffled strained conversation, one coming from inside the shower room. I stepped back away from the doorway. I strained my eyes in an attempt to make out if anyone was lurking in the shadows inside of the dark stall.

I grabbed my Maglite. I flashed the beam into the inky black room. The stalls were empty. There was nothing odd there. However, I knew I had heard something. My blood was pumping with adrenaline and I felt fear. I would have sworn there was someone talking in there. Still, the more I scanned the space, the less I heard. I chalked the noise up to just being the echo of an inmate's television.

So I continued making my rounds down Charlie and Delta walk. I made a mental note of the fact that no one was awake or talking. There were no televisions or radios on in any of the cells. Whatever the noise had been in the shower stall, there was no simple explanation for it. I reached the back of the hall and so was at the rear emergency door. I checked the fire exit door and then turned back around toward the entrance of the walk.

What I witnessed next was one of the most startling examples of an authentic haunting I had ever encountered. I stood transfixed, as an almost fully solid outline of a person began moving into the shower stall. Before I had time to react, a second and larger man-shape also floated across the walk floor into the stall.

I was concerned, of course, and frightened. Was I seeing an escape attempt or something else altogether, something of a supernatural nature? Was this activity something inhuman, maybe even something non-living? I couldn't stay trapped where I was. I knew that much. One had to pass the shower stall in order to get out of there. It was the only means of exit. Telling myself, I raced up the walk, not knowing just what I might be about to challenge, whether dangerous escaping criminals or otherwise... The front entrance next to the shower stall was obscured by a wall of darkness that seemed to bend the light around and away from the doorway. To me, it felt as if perhaps the phantasms, if that's what they were, could not bear the touch of light upon them. This anomaly played hell with my senses, though. I felt as if the room was shifting slowly, rotating to the left. I began to hear a high-pitched hum in my ears. A wave of nausea came over me.

I stopped moving forward for a moment. I let the skewed-seeming world settle back into order. I then turned toward the cells.

How in the hell can they sleep through all this going on around them? I thought, as I fought back the heavy feeling in my stomach that often came before the need to vomit. In another instant, the feeling subsided. I was able to move forward once again.

This had all taken about a minute it seemed to me, in order to reach the darkened shower area. My thoughts were electric during this. They were like sparks dancing around some faraday cage, dancing here and there, lighting on different subjects in quick succession. My mind was full of questions. Was it inmates, ones who had somehow broken free of their cells? As soon as I thought this, I dismissed the idea. I had seen through the figures. Besides, I would have heard a cell opening. At the very least, I should have seen any such escapees squeezing through cut bars.

I believed this was something else. I felt this was something paranormal.

What, I wondered, do I plan on doing if I find I've discovered two menacing transparent forms fighting in the shower? Do I call what may be an imprint from another time in to my supervisor as a fight? The idea seemed ludicrous to me. In any case, worrying about that part of things just didn't matter, at least, not beyond verifying what was awaiting me from inside that damp tiled hole in the wall.

I drew my Maglite and clicked it to life. I swung it out in front of me. I played a strong beam of light into the shower stall. I half expected to have at least one inmate on his back, possibly beaten to death. Perhaps the other was amped up and ready for me to enter. Maybe this was all an elaborate ruse of some sort to draw me in and I was going to be manhandled.

Neither scenario was one I looked forward to seeing come to fruition. I braced myself for whatever might come next. I aimed the tight white beam of light dead center of the shower. I moved the bright circle to all corners of the stall. I could see nothing there. I could still hear the faint strangled voice of a man in distress not more than three feet ahead of me in that shower room. Still, I saw nothing. I scanned the inner confines once again. I did this in case they had pressed up tight to the wall in order to avoid detection. There was no sign of any activity. Again, there was nothing.

The voices had at last begun to start fading. I searched the area immediately outside the shower for footprints. I hoped to find something to indicate anything other than what I believed I had just seen, some real evidence a real person had been here. I needed some kind of rational explanation. Anything I could use to bring some order to this event would help.

Failing to discover anything, I made a second round on my floor. Nothing was out of place anywhere. All the inmates were in their cells. I think I triple-checked every damned door lock and window on the floor that night. There was not a single thing to hint any sort of tampering had occurred. It was as if the event had never happened. There was not as much as a tinge of anything, dangerous or otherwise, present in the shower. I've to say, I was very thankful to see the sunrise that morning.

After leaving the penitentiary, I climbed into my van. I turned the key in the ignition. The engine sputtered to life with low and steady rumble. The wipers' back-and-forth motion cleared the heavy dew blocking my view through the windshield. I rubbed my eyes, I felt drained from the experience.

I was out of sorts on my drive home. I had taken the long way, feeling I needed time to get the event out of my head before I arrived home and had to go into "daddy-mode." I gripped the steering wheel, appreciating the rock solid, absolute reality of it. I needed something tangible I could use to tether myself to the "normal" world. After an hour of burning gas, I was able to relegate the prison events to the "weird crap file" I kept in my brain and head on home.

Some days passed since the event. I found myself again working as the Second Floor Walk Officer. I had mentioned the paranormal occurrence to the inmate janitor who now lived on

Echo walk. He had been at the Kentucky State Penitentiary for nearly 50 years. He had an intimate knowledge of the prison's lore.

The janitor was not thrilled talking about this kind of subject matter. He had to sleep there at night. He had become religious in his later years. He was now a "dyed in the wool" Christian who believed that the dead did not speak. However, after pressing him, he did open up about what he knew.

He said, "There are indeed spirits there. Charlie and Delta walk shower was one of the most haunted places in Kentucky State Penitentiary." That is saying something for a facility of its type.

The janitor went on to explain he had stayed in after the let-out. He was finishing up with some hall cleaning. The man told me there had been two inmates. There had been some bad blood between them. One of the inmates in question lived on Alpha Bravo walk. The other had lived on Echo walk. Both men had known one another before coming to The Kentucky State Penitentiary. They had always been close friends up until then, with neither having had any real run-in with the other before then.

One time, the men had been on painting work detail all week for an upcoming American Correctional Association and Standards inspection. The ACA is a health and safety organization that tours KSP every few years. They do safety reviews of the prison. The KSP administrative branch wanted even the toilets to have a high shine on them. The stress of all this can make for a very tense time for everyone.

The maintenance staff attended to most of the major revamps and structural repairs in Five Cell House. The remainder of what was left was detail work. This, among all the other nickel-and-dime stuff was painting, and lots of it. It was rather like putting lipstick on a pig, but it was how the Kentucky State Penitentiary wanted it.

It was not clear if the two men's dispute had been over money, or drugs, or perhaps some form of disrespect to each other. Whatever the cause, the dispute came to a head that one night. The drama started after the general population lock-up. However, after some name-calling and threats occurring, the trash-talk seemed to be over. The two men were later let out of their cells to go on a painting detail on the morning shift.

The walk officer working that night was not aware of the previous issues day. He had allowed the two inmates to move without restraint on the walks. At first, the various job assignments kept them separated. Their hands were occupied for a time. A good number of the jobs were completed without incident. One of the jobs included a fresh coat of paint on the interior of the shower stall on Charlie and Delta walk.

Then, as they worked closer together, tempers flared up once again. This time, threats became physical violence. The weaker of the two men soon realized he could not defend himself and had to flee. He made a failed attempt to run back to his cell. He slipped on the wet floor and fell at the front of the Charlie and Delta walk shower.

The weaker one was dazed and semi-conscious as he tried to pull himself up by means of the cell's bars. The stronger inmate was still in pursuit. He tripped and tumbled over the weaker inmate. This enraged him so much, he seemed to have a psychotic episode. He grabbed and then pulled the weaker one into the shower stall.

Screams carried throughout the cell house. This noise caused the whole place to go into an uproar, and then there was chaos. The other inmates were tossing mattresses around in their cells. The angry inmates littered the walk with anything they could find in their cells. This took place on every walk. Furthermore, this mayhem distracted the officer's attention from the job detail.

Before the walk officer could react and reach the walk, the attack was over. The larger inmate had already stabbed the other to death with one of the large, sharpened paint scrapers they had for the job. When the overwhelmed walk officer finally arrived at the shower room. He came upon a garish sight. The walls had been splattered with blood. Gore smeared the lime-green tiles.

"It was like a God-damned slaughter house inside of there, Cap," the old inmate recounted. He also added, "That was the reality of Maggie's back then. The prison could turn on you like a sleeping bear waking up in a heartbeat."

The janitor's story rang true. As a paranormal investigator, I believe what I experienced that night on the walk was residual energy. This, for me, was a classic haunting. The power of that murderous event set in place a looping replay of that dark moment. I then later witnessed an event.

CHAPTER 7

THE THIRTEENTH STEP

"*Twelve knots turned with hate, but the thirteenth knot will seal your fate.*" This line was like some dark nursery rhyme that Victorian children might sing as they played in a grassy field. In the early years of The Kentucky State Penitentiary, things were Spartan. Life in the wake of a post-Confederate South was desolate. Their armies lay destroyed. Their food stocks emptied. The economy was in a shambles.

This was the lowest point in the South's history. Conditions were third world. Kentucky had suffered the most. Many of their towns were in ruins. Little help came from the North. Life was, indeed, bleak. The population had been demoralized. The Confederate money was worthless and this further threw the South into abject poverty. Many families were without any means of support and they were starving. People provided for themselves any way they could. Often this was by means of crime.

In the time long before the advent of the now-infamous electric chair, the state's choice in matters of execution was the hangman's noose. People had little trust in the newly rebuilt southern government. Any serious crime meets with the harshest and most direct of consequences. Those in power pushed for tough and final solutions to crime.

STEVE E. ASHER

The list of crimes that one could hang for ran the gamut of everything from horse theft to arson, rape to murder, or even incest. These things were even more likely to get you to swing in the hangman's noose if you happened to be a person of color. Those were times of high inequality in early Kentucky. The racial divide was never more evident or more poisonous in its nature and extent.

More recently, Anthony, who was a native New Yorker, had worked most of his life in construction. He had always been the first one to pitch in on a project. He had a pleasant demeanor. His arms and face always turned red from exposure to the sun and the harsh elements. He worked as a laborer for a construction company and as a bricklayer.

Anthony grew up in a factory-worker family. The skills he gained early on came from his father and uncles. There was not much time for fun and games in those mean streets. Either one got to work or one had to get out. His father passed away that summer from lung cancer. After his father's death, his interest in the steel industry all but dried up.

Anthony sold off what he could not pack into his truck. He traveled south. He found work on a roofing crew in Eddyville, Kentucky, before meeting Tandy, who later talked him into looking into working at the prison. The two eventually started seeing each other. They both agreed to give KSP a two-year trial. If he could start the furniture shop he wanted by then, he would quit the prison. While waiting to get on at the prison, he read about the place, studied its history. He could see why some felt the place might be haunted. Once he was at the penitentiary, he began to see things were, in fact, quite strange there.

He was to working in the yard one evening. He was supposed to search for contraband when the inmates were inside the cell houses. Contraband could be anything from weapons to drugs, and even smuggled cell phones.

Kentucky's hard rains and thunderstorms accent the fall season. This meant the yard was muddy, wet, and slick, so Anthony stood on the game deck. Now, he was relaxing a bit and admiring the prison's architecture, although still keeping a watchful eye from the top of the hill, beneath the shelter of the small pavilion.

This site was where the inmates would often play dominoes or sit around and roll cigarettes, or perhaps gambled and thus wasted the better part of their day. In a place like the prison, either you had time, or time had you. It was best to "busy" your hands before something found a way to busy them for you. Most inmates preferred not to do this, and tended to make poor life choices, so they found trouble as a result.

The spot around the pavilion seemed to resonate with Anthony in some weird way. He could not articulate what the feelings were. "Fear" was the word that would come to mind if he had been asked to label the sensation. There always seemed to be an oppressive force on that hilltop. He knew that seemed crazy, yet it was true. After a few minutes of standing there, he went on to handle his other duties, and then went home for the evening.

Anthony woke from what he thought must have been a nightmare. He could not remember any of the dream, though. All that remained was the unease of whatever thing had happened in his nightmare. He decided to try to clear his head by going outside to his small workshop.

Mr. Griggs was the old man who lived across the way from Anthony. He had overheard Anthony tapping and banging one day. He walked over and saw Anthony moving some things around in the makeshift workshop.

"Care for a hand, young man?" Mr. Griggs asked. Anthony gave him a nod. He was trying to install an overhead florescent light in the center of the room. He wanted to have better light in the spot where he planned doing the bulk of his detailed woodwork.

Within fifteen minutes, the light was up and secured in place. He thanked Mr. Griggs by offering him a cold drink. The old man opted for some of Tandy's iced sun tea and something to eat.

After the meal, Griggs touched on the fact he had been a guard at the prison. At one point, the old man asked him in a hushed tone, "So have you seen anything sort of off yet?"

Anthony spoke of the odd feelings, and of even having heard a disembodied voice once.

Griggs nodded and said, "When you see something really off, you'll know." Anthony's next shift came and went without incident. He also worked his day off. Due to the violence of the job, KSP had massive amounts of people that leave. The place has a high turnover in labor force. This meant overtime for those who wanted it.

That evening, Anthony arrived home from work. He thought he'd spend a little quiet time on the back deck. He used this precious time to clear his head of all the crap he dealt with during his time on his shifts at the prison.

He considered all the stories he had been told about the place, what had been seen and heard by other officers there. These just had not happened to him, at least not yet. He started to doubt some of the accounts as fantasy, and so tended to dismiss their veracity.

His next shift, he was again working the yard by seeing to the kitchen detail. Anthony had to help escort the last of the kitchen workers across the top of the hill to Six Cell House for the night lock-in. After announcing on his radio to six and ten wall stands of his intentions, he then unlocked the gate as the tired men filed along. He finally had all the inmates secured within the cell house. At this point, Anthony had paused and taken a second to collect himself, before heading back to the count office. To relax, he leaned against the dull brick wall there. A low fog was moving onto the yard. This was a river mist, the kind of dense fog that forms close to open bodies of water at night. The general atmosphere and look of the place made him feel as if he was on set of an old Hammer Films horror movie. The wall of creeping cloud made the prison appear even more like some creepy old castle.

He knew his moment's respite was limited, for Anthony was sure he would soon get a quick call, a "Hey you—go over to Four Cell House and toss some cells. Make sure to check for some contraband." He'd heard such a command often enough before.

This sort of mission was captain-speak for "I do not want you in my office all night drinking coffee and farting around. You all need something to go do."

Anthony had no problem with this, He was used to being outside and on the move, or active in some way or other.

As he approached the barbwire-topped fences encompassing ten-wall stand, he became aware of something odd. He started to hear a strange rapping sound. Anthony assumed this was just a woodpecker working in a nearby tree, and he was hearing the echo. That, after all, was the probability, although his intuition told him otherwise.

Anthony went as far as to walk up to the pavilion and check all of the legs of the picnic tables. Often inmates hid things like small knives there for protection, in case of a riot on the yard. While, he did this, Anthony searched for alternatives to the phantom sound, since he was now convinced this was no woodpecker. He looked inside the large metal trash barrels. He thought, perhaps, there was a can in a bag that could be hanging loosely, maybe causing that double tapping. He again found nothing. As the sound continued to manifest the noise disturbed him even more.

He could see the fog moving past the lower part of the prison wall. The mist had cloaked the ground.

The noise continued. *What the hell is that?* he wondered. There was nothing out here to make such a sound. The noise was not metallic in nature, but rather was a slow, steady wooden thud. The sound went on like this, only to make long pauses and start up again. He decided to give up for the night and go on to the office, because his search seemed pointless. The unknown noise faded away to nothing in the cool night air as he moved away from the pavilion.

Once at the Count Office, he did get a new work assignment. Anthony spent the rest of the evening in Four Cell House helping inventory the property of an inmate that was guilty of contraband. He escorted the inmate and his possessions to Three Cell House lock-up once the chore was completed.

With the shift over, Anthony wasted no time in getting out of there. He was in his trusty Ford F-150 in a matter of minutes. He sped through the dense fog toward home. He wanted to see his girlfriend and get away from "Spookville, USA." The touch of the wet fog seeping into his cracked open window seemed somehow different outside of the prison's influence. The heavy quality now absent from the mist. He still had the nagging concern as to what he had dealt with back at the prison.

"Was it real, and if so, what did that noise mean?" he asked himself, as he sped along the narrow country road toward his house.

The short time working at the prison had shown him things he had never seen before. None seemed more bizarre than what he had experienced that night. As he drifted off to sleep, he remembered what his neighbor, Mr. Griggs, had said: "You will know it when you hear it. You will just know."

Things stayed quiet over the next few months. The trees were devoid of leaves. Tandy's workload lessened and the prison promised Anthony a move to whatever shift he preferred, and so the next week, he made the move to the night shift.

Anthony had all but forgotten "the night of the phantom knocking." There were enough real and tangible threats at the prison to keep him busy already, without his worrying about the paranormal ones.

On the first night of the new shift, his focus was on assisting the maintenance crew. The yard property room needed repairs. There was a leak in the wall facing the hillside. The place always had water running down the walls this time of year.

He posted himself to the top, at the pavilion. It had rained hard that day. The ground was saturated and slick underfoot. The first signs of a freeze were heralded in the form of a cold north wind.

He could hear the maintenance staff below him, pissing and moaning to one another, as usual. He watched as the small maintenance crew, now finished, loaded the remainder of their tools inside of the storage building beneath the pavilion. They did not lock the door. They just walked down the track toward the shop.

It was then Anthony again heard the familiar sound. The rapping noise, that gentle yet persistent knocking, had returned once more. Some time had passed since he had first heard the sounds. He recognized them as the same noise he dealt with before. The disturbing "tap-tap-tap" continued this. He started counting these raps. They always went to 13 before hesitating and then starting over again.

Anthony walked around the top of the pavilion, searching for the source of the sounds. He wanted some sort of explanation, something rooted in some form of rational logic.

Anthony, alone now, could see that the lights of the maintenance room were still on. This meant the crew had not been the source of the strange noise, which continued. Something else, something strange was going on. Mr. Griggs would have said, "Something was off."

Anthony later said he felt as though some power wanted him down in the yard. Although he couldn't describe this feeling precisely, he knew for certain he had to get off that pavilion; that is, if he wanted any chance of locating where the mysterious noised emanated from. He reached the bottom of the darkened staircase. He looked to see if there was any sort of activity in the yard that could account for the strange knocking. Anthony found nothing amiss.

The area adjacent to the pavilion had a queer-looking haze rising. This oddity rolled forward and cast off an almost backlight effect. The mist folded and twisted in on itself and then gained a semi-solid look to it. Anthony stared. He didn't believe his eyes. He looked away for but a moment, blinked to clear his eyes, and looked again.

The phenomenon now appeared as a moving mass. The terrifying apparition moved over the top of the hill, and toward the staircase, he had just descended. He tried to scream, but couldn't.

The odd thought struck him that while he had wanted to see something paranormal, this certainly was not what he had expected, not something on this scale. Anthony stepped back, away from the thing, whatever it was. He pressed his body flat up against the wall of the yard office. A putrid smell, which he had become aware of earlier, now increased. This caused a surge of terror that made his stomach pitch in offense.

Now, and despite himself and his terror, as if compelled, Anthony inched closer to the thing. There was a pressure building in his head as he did this, similar to what one might experience when taking off in a plane or driving through the high mountains—a sort of pressure change. The faintest music came with the sensation.

The music sounded very old, out of date and was reminiscent of a Negro spiritual. There was a distinct mournful sound to the music, a sense of pure sadness. This was anguish beyond words. This was blood out of a wound and tears from a battered eye. The tap, tap, tapping still could be heard, along with the solemn music. The tedious voices in the tune built in intensity. Anthony stood within six feet of the base of the stairs where the strange anomaly drifted. The activity joined with a reverberant rattling. Now he heard a distinct rattling and clanking sound, one reminiscent of the sound iron shackles made when moved. Still, he inched ever closer to the apparition. He was desperate to stop his advance, but his legs would not heed his mental commands. He glanced about him, seeking aid in a wild search for help. There was no one else about. He was alone in his nightmare world.

He watched as the churning mass drifted upward, mounted the stairs.

The advancing mass seemed to overtake and engulf the stairs. A bitter cold pierced Anthony's back, as if somehow the icy thing has pierced his soul. Anthony felt as if his legs were about to buckle, and yet, he couldn't seem to fall.

Then he gasped for air, for it was as if someone had punched him hard in his stomach. Anthony could see a figure rise out of his torso. By this point, he was in utter shock. The twisting shape emerged farther from his body. The growing lower strip formed long ribbons of sour-smelling, greasy matter that resembled thin and spindle-like arms.

The dark spurting fluid left his chest. It wound upward and danced about in a terrifying display. The ribbons converged then separated, only to converge yet again, as if made of some supernatural putty. Anthony could feel his energy leaving his body. He felt drained. The ectoplasm, for he realized this was what he must be seeing, coalesced. The black mass began to take on a definable shape.

The pavilion faded into the inky background as the thing became more solid in appearance. There was the menacing outline, a gallows. He felt the dark emanation of arcane power.

Its maddening, all-consuming hunger drew him in. The force demanded sacrifice and it meant to have it right now. The black thread vibrated and pulled Anthony forward.

The entity was still connected to Anthony's chest by a series of dark hanging strings and these pulled him forward, made him walk as if on command. However, the strange being seemed oblivious to Anthony or what he was experiencing. The shadowy phantom moved forward toward the hazy spirit construction. Anthony watched as the gaunt-appearing apparition glided toward the base of the spectral scaffolding. Scrawny arms appeared to be wearing shackles. Only the upper portion of the specter's body showed. There was only vapor, a mist, or a smoke-like cloud where the legs should have been.

No gallows had been at the prison for a long time. This image had to be from a period long past. Although vague and lacking sharpness, Anthony felt as if he was watching some old film on abusive policies of early Kentucky prisons, as he later would describe the event. The music was still there and now, if anything, was more robust. The melody made him want to weep and yet he had no tears that would come. The "other" still seemed to have full command of Anthony's actions.

The singing had now ballooned into a cacophony. There were wails and jeering noises from apparently phantasmal convicts, now long gone. There was also the sound of the heavy "TAP, TAP, TAP." He watched the pitiful figure, slumped over as it climbed the spectral stairs.

When the figure reached the thirteenth step, Anthony felt control of his body returning to him. As he regained possession of himself, he witnessed the wretched shadow of a now long-dead man walk to the middle of the shadowy platform. The forsaken soul then turned to face Anthony's direction. He peered up into the doomed man's shadowed eyes and saw the hopelessness they conveyed.

Though Anthony could see no other figure on that haunted gallows, he watched with a dark horror, as a disembodied noose appeared on the scaffolding. The braided rope teased the spectral rabble in attendance. Anthony tried to force a scream through gritted teeth, but could not. Nothing escaped his lips. He stood, literally paralyzed with fear. His eyes stayed locked on the unfolding tragedy. Above the singing, he could hear thunderous catcalls. A shadowy trap door swung down. The dismal spirit dropped through the platform. Then, the tortured vision disappeared from sight, simply vanished in an instant. Anthony felt the spirit filaments, which had still been attached to his chest, give way. As the ectoplasm ripped from his chest, he could hear a sickening, sucking *pop*. Freed at last, Anthony, as if a puppet with its strings cut, collapsed hard to the ground.

He lay there, stunned. The monotonous "tap, tap, tap" sound had abruptly ceased. All the eerie noised faded out of existence. Only the sound of rain and then the noise of approaching footsteps could be heard.

Anthony felt himself lifted into the air. Panicked, he fought. Then a voice, one Anthony recognized as that of the maintenance supervisor, said, "Take it easy, boy. You had one hell of a spill. Must have knocked yourself clean out. Those damn stairs are killers."

The maintenance men helped Anthony to his feet. He was soaked and shivering from lying on the wet ground. Another man had come. He wrapped Anthony in a gray-wool, army blanket. The men then took him to the prison hospital to have his head looked at.

Anthony had suffered a few small cuts and bruises. Overall, though, he was not seriously hurt. He did not have a concussion. However, he did go home to recuperate.

Anthony recovered in a matter of a few days. He sported a small lump behind his ears for at least another two weeks. He did not tell his captain what had happened. They thought he had fallen. Moreover, they acted as if this is what they wanted to hear, rather than some fantastic tale.

Anthony, at the time, had also decided to let Tandy keep thinking he had just slipped, as well. He did not want to disturb her with his waking nightmare, or whatever it had been. The prison administrators moved him back to day shift upon his return to the penitentiary. He stayed assigned to the yard for a good part of his time there, but the haunting never occurred again. For this, Anthony was very thankful. He and his girl stuck to the plan of saving up some money. Within two years, he had left the prison for good.

The new wood shop did well enough. Both he and Tandy were meeting their bills. They even were able to save a little, enough to open the furniture business full-time. However, Anthony never forgot that night at the prison. Furthermore, he had no doubt it had been a real event. "When you know, you will just know," he muttered to himself in his wood shop one day, quoting the now-departed Mr. Griggs. Anthony rubbed the small scar just behind his ear as he did this. This was a permanent souvenir from his time at KSP, and that horrible night. He gave a light shudder and then went back to work. Anthony could now shrug off what happened, but he could never forget, as he later told me.

CHAPTER 8

DON'T LOOK UP

Violence is a mainstay of life inside of most institutions. The vast majority of inmates tend to try to and maintain peace between themselves and the guards. There are times tensions become too high for civility. This is when bad things happen. When the inmates feel like they had been mistreated is when all hell breaks loose. This may be a minor thing, as a work stoppage, or as major as a full-scale riot.

A good friend and supervisor submitted this next occurrence to me from Kentucky State Penitentiary. His name is Dan.

There had been a riot at another institution up in Northern Kentucky. The destruction that had taken place was massive. There was millions of dollars' worth of damage. Several of the buildings there burned and many of those inmates had been transferred to KSP. The prison has always received the problems of other places in its long, one hundred plus years in business. This latest situation was to be no different.

The day of the mass move was pure chaos. The influx of transfers went on throughout the day and then well into the night. The penitentiary stays filled close to its maximum occupancy. The new inmates had to sleep in various locations in the prison as a result. There were not enough cells to hold all of them in the cell houses. The new inmates knew they had to make the best of it. Luckily, the additional inmates suffered little from the move. There was a time when this was not always so.

In the penitentiary's history, when there was this kind of overcrowding, terrible conditions had led to the outbreak of disease. In the past, scurvy and tuberculosis swept through the castle like a creeping death. The bodies were then stacked up like stones, waiting disposal by the overworked staff. The overwhelming smell of decaying bodies was a constant and terrible thing.

However, this sort of level of inmate mortality had changed a lot since those times. However, many paranormal experts believe that events such as mass deaths can cause an increase in the likelihood of future haunting or spectral activity. In addition, the Kentucky State Penitentiary had seen more deaths than any now functioning institutions in the commonwealth.

As the introduction of these transferred prisoners occurred, many of the new inmates had to find a place to sleep in the recreation building overnight. The inmates housed in the sports center slept on low cots, or at worst, slept on thin mattresses along the indoor basketball court. Many of the new inmates had arrived on a Friday. Most of them had brought very little to eat. The hour was too late for any of them to buy anything at the canteen. They all ate in the prison kitchen those first few days. This was a simple meal of sandwiches and juice for the transferred prisoners.

The men then went back to their assigned spots in the Recreation Building after eating. Dan was the yard supervisor on the second night the transfers stayed in the old gym. He had to escort an inmate back to the recreation building from the kitchen. The inmate was diabetic and needed to rest because he had elevated blood sugar. Dan signaled to the wall stands his intentions of escorting the man.

They walked past the slop dock and down the edge of the walking track. He heard the inmate mutter something along the lines of, "That place is hot down there."

Dan was not certain of the exact words the inmate had said, and so asked him to repeat it.

The inmate looked at him and then pointed toward the old recreation building. He said, "I said that place is haunted down here, cap."

This comment piqued Dan's interest, so he pressed him to say more by asking, "Do you care to explain what you mean?" He wanted to hear just what had this man feeling so scared. He could see the unease on the inmate's face. Dan waited patiently as the inmate visibly gathered his courage.

Finally, the man said, "You know how your guard key ring will jingle as you walk around on rounds." The anxious inmate then added, "Well, I heard something just like it late last night, Cap. It was after lock-up, inside that building."

Dan had never been what one would call a religious man. This was even truer of holding any beliefs in things thought of as paranormal. His outlook was: "Facts are facts. Anything else is hearsay." That said, this still was an unusual thing to hear from an inmate.

Dan, half-joking, asked, "Well, what makes you think there was a ghost, or something dark?"

The inmate replied, "I was lying on my bunk. I hadn't been able to sleep very well. Maybe, it was because I was in a new place, but I could not get past this odd feeling. I had the sense I wasn't alone. I had just lain down after taking a piss when I heard something like keys rattling. I assumed one of your yard officers had come to do a walk through and to check on me. I thought I would see a guard. I didn't."

Dan could see the inmate was shaken by the memory. Both Dan and the inmate neared the building now. Dan stopped walking long enough to finish his cigarette, and to let the inmate finish telling what he had seen.

Dan could clearly see the trepidation showing in the inmate's face. The man's eyes were wide. Dan had seen this look before. Often, the inmates that had served time in isolation for a year or more were very skittish and fearful once released. They had this look.

Then, the inmate closed his eyes and seemed to steady his now rapid breathing. This was an attempt to regain some self-control, Dan was sure.

The inmate then said, "I heard the sound of hard-soled shoes clicking on the floor and noises that were like swinging keys getting closer to me. I felt a sharp spike in temperature and all of this, in a matter of seconds. The strangest thing is that no one was there. The sound suddenly stopped. Then, I felt like I was in an icebox. This was then I saw him."

Dan listened intently now. He could hear the fear in the inmate's voice. Whatever the activity was, it scared this man. "That's a hell of a story, son," Dan commented.

"There is more to tell you, Captain. I don't want you to think you're talking to a whack job," the inmate said.

Dan assured the inmate he passed no judgment on him, and then said, "All right then. Let me have the rest of what happened. What's the worst this could be?"

The prisoner said, "I lay there trying to be as still as I could in hopes this spirit or demon would pass on by me. The thing was almost on top of me. I could feel it. Cap. I couldn't stop myself. It was driving me crazy not knowing what was haunting me.

"That was when I opened my eyes. It wasn't a man, Not a living one anyway, by the looks of it, but it looked like a guard."

Dan could not come to grips with what he had heard. "A dead guard?" What the hell was the man trying to say? "You saw a ghost officer?"

The inmate stared at the door to the building with a distinct foreboding. "Yeah. That ghost guard had a cold blank expression. The body was transparent. I could tell the thing wasn't a modern officer. He was in an old, antique, sort of guard uniform." The clothes were like something worn in that movie, *The Green Mile*. It was a hell of a sight. This guard seemed real, at least until I looked down below the waist. And the thing's hands were missing. The arms just ended in blunted stumps. From the knees down, the body just seemed to fade away to nothing, kind of like faint wisps of smoke or something.

The inmate paused, and then added, "The one thing I remember most was his eyes. They were milky white and they never blinked once." The inmate then told Dan he watched as the spirit began to advance on him. The phantasm then moved over and through the wall of the inmate's bunk. The convict buried his head into his pillow to muffle his screams of terror. He then lay on his bunk trembling with fear for a long time, too scared to move at all, let alone leave his bunk.

Once the sun was up, the prisoner spent the remainder of the day of the event outside. He stayed as far away from the building as he could.

Having heard the dread tale, now Dan was infected with a certain apprehension, as well. There had been truth in the inmate's voice about what had manifested. Dan could tell the inmate had not just been spinning a tale for the hell of it, to screw with him. As far as the convict was concerned, Dan had no doubt the man believed he had encountered something inexplicable. Even though this was against prison rules, Dan now gave the inmate a cigarette to calm him. He was still quite uncomfortable with the idea of staying in that building again overnight, which to Dan's way of thinking was understandable.

Still, Dan was a logical man. He had heard strange stories before, weird conversations whispered between officers and inmates alike of such things occurring at the prison.

As a paranormal researcher, I believe many of us learn to ignore or un-see certain types of paranormal activity. Those new to a location may have no such safeguards. They go inside of those walls with no filter to entities that may choose to manifest to them.

Dan said, "That was one hell of a story. I've never seen anything like that at the prison. I hope I never have to see a ghost, either."

For the inmate, Dan finally unlocked the recreation building for the inmate to go inside. The prisoner shuddered at the sound of the jingling keys as Dan did so.

Dan had to ask one final question. "If you hear the sound again tonight, what are you going to do about it?"

"Well..." The inmate paused, thought on this a moment, and said, "I'm going to turn my face toward the wall and not look up. No way am I looking up and seeing that thing again."

As far as I know, no other incidents occurred with the phantasm. While still working at the penitentiary, I had attempted to get the inmate to speak about all of this, but he had steadfastly refused. He was a short-timer and so had less than a year before he was to leave. He wanted to "just do his time" without any unwanted attention.

After Dan told me this story, he asked for my opinion on what the inmate had seen. My belief is that what the inmate had experienced was a residual haunting and I told Dan this.

Many paranormal experts say that, many times, a segment of time is in a loop. This loop then replays itself for an indefinite period, and so is referred to as a "repeater." The shadowy specter goes about doing whatever chore it did in life, over and over. The vision is a sort of echo that is either not aware, or at least remains unaware of anyone else that may be watching it. I believe most cases of hauntings are of this repeater variety.

If pressed for advice on handling some strange noise or play of light in the hallway, this is my suggestion: The next time someone is alone at night and then thinks they hear a knock, tap, or rattle down the hall or sees a swirling shadow, or feel a chill even on a hot night, DO NOT LOOK UP! From everything I've gathered, they are much safer that way.

CHAPTER 9

THE MOTHERLESS SON

There are some generalized truths most people have of prisoners. The first one is the stereotypical caricature of a hoodlum. They see convicts always as rough-cut and looking like they have just stepped out of the pages of some old detective book. Most often, they are thought of as looking murderous and cruel. They are seen as creatures that live only to rape and pillage, and they hold no redeeming qualities whatsoever.

The second myth people have clung to goes as follows: Inmates are all mean and subhuman creatures. They are monsters devoid of any kind of moral compass. They have neither the motivation nor the education to be anything more. Dim and apt to behaving without conscience, they are secondary citizens of the worst ilk. They deserve whatever treatment befalls them.

One can go to the prison today and find inmates that would fit that role as if they were straight out of central casting. In reality, they are the few. There are trends in criminality just as in anything. For example, when was the last time anyone heard about a train robbery?

One could consider whether continued exposure to high levels of stress coupled with paranormal activity can amplify prison mania. I am a former correctional officer, as well as a researcher of the paranormal, and I think this does, based on all the evidence I've seen and my long-term personal experiences.

Criminal intent and confinement sometimes are the catalyst for true horror. It is important to understand at least a bit of the history of the penitentiary's early years for this reason. Those years were both turbulent, and a blight on Kentucky as a whole.

The Kentucky State Penitentiary was essentially an asylum of sorts. The year was 1884. Then Kentucky governor, Luke P. Blackburn, appropriated the necessary funds to build a modern penitentiary at Eddyville, Kentucky. That is, modern by the standards of the day. This was a political favor to his friend and Eddyville native son, General H.B. Lyon.

What Lyon had on his hands was nothing short of a cruel sweatbox. It was built on the yoke of free inmate labor, and harsh mistreatment. KSP was a state-mandated, slave shack for human chattel. The life of a prisoner was often short and terrible in the extreme. The conditions were nothing short of barbaric.

It should be remembered that some inmates were no more than eleven or twelve years of age. By today's standards, these were clearly minors. Often those children had to fend off the abuse and sexual advances of true predators for hours on end, if they could manage it at all. What kind of a hell this must have been for them? They found no compassion, escape, or forgiveness. There was only torment for those lost souls. Those motherless sons died alone, uncared for, and unwanted, except by sexual predators, of course. One cannot imagine this happening today.

Some paranormal experts believe the dead come and go without fear. They can appear wherever and whenever they feel like. If so, what dark arcane powers can these spirits hold over the living? If a spirit of a young child were in a prison, would there be anything to fear from the living? Have you ever seen an enraged child? Now give that child the freedom from the confinement of a human body. Imagine the havoc they could wreak, if they so choose under such conditions.

A woman by the name of Kay remembers crossing the Kentucky state line in the first week of November. She was behind the wheel of her 1979 VW Beetle convertible. She had the car's faded top down. She was enjoying the uncharacteristically warm day. She had her auburn shoulder length hair pulled back like a fiery ponytail. The sun felt soothing against her skin. Little did Kay know what was in store for her in Kentucky.

Kay loved her car. It was one of the few things she had kept from before the "sad event" went down. This was the term her mother, Carol, used when referring to the bad separation of Kay from her husband. Kay grew up in Evansville, Indiana. She had decided to move south to escape her past and the gossip about her life back in her home state.

She put rent down on a little cheap apartment in Eddyville, Kentucky. The sparse dwelling was clean and small. The house was scant five-minute drive to the lake. Her first day at the lake was when she saw The Kentucky State Penitentiary. The dark castle of a prison loomed in the distance. It didn't take her long to learn about some of the murderous history and the dark dealings within those Gothic-style walls.

Most people in the town either lived close to the prison, because they worked there, or because they had family either working or serving time there. There were few people in the area whose lives were not in some way connected to the prison. Kay was equally affected. When she was not filling out job applications, she seemed to find herself always drawn to the prison. That sprawling castle had a way of captivating a person.

As a paranormal researcher, I believe that places that may hold strong spiritual energy and may emanate a sort of pulse that resonates with many people. This is not something most people can explain adequately in words. They just "feel" it, and are drawn to the source. For instance, I often worked in the wall stands on dayshift. I frequently saw people from all over the country that came to take pictures of the "Castle on the Cumberland." When I asked why they came so far for this purpose, they could only explain they felt "drawn" there.

Kay spent her initial weeks in Eddyville at her job, which was wrapping bouquets at the flower shop. Off hours, she would read. She had always held an interest in those things paranormal. As a result, Kay spent a lot of time reading about haunted locations.

She had shown signs in pre-adolescence of a latent paranormal ability. Her budding gift began with feeling things that others could not. This went beyond an imaginary friend that small children may conjure up, or the occasional shadow person in a corner late at night. It seemed to her that the dead would actually sought her out.

By early December, she had met a few of the penitentiary guards through the florist shop. One of them mentioned the prison was always hiring. However, Kay had no desire to get into that line of work, but she needed money. Finally, and reluctant to do so, she filled out an application for work at the prison.

Having studied the history of the prison, and given her interest in the paranormal, Kay knew there might be a risk working in the prison environment. Still, she didn't let this sway her in her need to work there.

By the end of May she had had completed both her first and second interviews successfully. Kay was now a thirty-something rookie officer. She had been part of a big mass hire. The first time she ventured inside the heavy inner gates and out to the prison yard, she felt an indefinable sadness connected to the place. The feeling was not overwhelming and so she put it aside. Kay was there to work and that was all. She didn't want to become involved with the living, let alone the dead. It was not that she didn't want any friends, but it was just that relationships became complicated quickly, and after her breakup, she was in no hurry to establish new relationships.

Kay arrived home from work one raining spring afternoon. She caught sight of a small package sitting just outside her door. Kay had received a small manila folder by mail from her mother. There were letters written in heavy black marker. The folder read in bold print "Your memories." Inside were things she had left back at her mother's garage in Evansville.

Kay had no plans to immediately open the package. She had other things she wished to do. After doing everything she felt she needed to, she settled on the love seat. The manila folder loomed there on the table before her. For some reason, this felt like some dark omen to her, a form of a Pandora's Box.

What pox hast ye so vexed me with this day, dear mother? Kay thought, laughing to herself.

Yet, with some apprehension, she picked up the package, worked at the tape there until it freed its grip on the thick envelope.

The package held various miscellaneous items like an old photo of her and her grandma in happier times. There were other snapshots, as well. There were even some of her report cards from when she was very young. She neared the bottom of the package. Hidden in amongst them was the true reason her mother had sent what amounted to a Trojan horse. Opening the tiny velour lined box, Kay found her wedding band. Kay put it aside. That part of her life was over.

Kay stayed at the prison for some time. While there, she worked at various posts, including the wall stands and places with less inmate contact. By this time, five years had passed since she had first hired in at The Kentucky State Penitentiary. Kay was then working on evening shift in the administration control center. Her break was nearly through when Kay heard the captain call out for her.

"Kay, are you still on your break?"

She saw him poke his balding head around the corner of the count office door. Kay downed the last of the coffee. She then rose and went to see what "Mr. Grumbles," as she thought of him, wanted.

"I've a proposition for you, gal," the captain said.

Kay gave him a deadpan look.

"I want you to switch out with a yard officer, and help go through mail," he explained.

This was something new. She had never been able to get beyond control centers or wall stands. The dayshift officer assigned to the mailroom had been out sick due to a nasty case of the stomach flu. The captain went on to explain she would have a lieutenant there to oversee the work. She would be running the mailbags to all of the cell houses. Kay was all for this. She would take any chance to explore a little.

She soon found out just why she had this glorious assignment. There were literally piles of letters to go through. They covered half of the floor. Inmates get enormous amounts of mail, because it is often their main means of communication with friends and family in the outside world. The lieutenant that night was new to his rank. His name was Taylor. Together they began sifting through the ocean of mail left behind by the ailing staffer.

They had sorted through maybe a tenth of the mountain of parcels at one point. Kay sat at the far wall, facing the hallway door. The entranceway was open to try to capitalize on some of the breeze wafting up into the building's left wing. The mailroom was located just past the control center in the administration office that received the occasional odd gust. The hallway between the mailroom and the control center has a locked metal hatch in the floor. This was an area known as "the dungeons," a name given to a room buried beneath several feet of concrete and steel. The dungeon was a room once used to torture inmates in the early years of the institution.

By the time I worked for the state of Kentucky, this had been all but forgotten. The one time I saw it opened, the chains that had bound inmates still hung from the walls there.

Kay let out a half-chuckle, one that seemed to surprise Taylor. This was because she was also a ghost of sorts. Kay realized something strange had come over her, that the laugh had sounded out of character, even to herself, but now, she quickly regained her composure. Shaking off the odd if fleeting sensation, she turned her attention back to the work. She had finished her next stack when she caught movement just beyond the office doorway. An odd shadow seemed to have slipped by.

She had seen it for but a moment, but had seemed more than just a mere shadow, a chance trick of the light. There had been a sort of substance to it, an ethereal and grayish-looking haze, but it had disappeared as quickly as it had come. It was gone from her sight almost as soon as it had appeared. Kay's attempt to rationalize this event didn't work. This visitation, or whatever one wanted to call it, had felt real on a visceral level. She tried to keep her concern private, not let on she'd seen anything. However, in secret, she was beside herself with fear and anxiety.

Taylor must have been speaking to her for several seconds without her responding.

He at last gained her attention with a forceful: "Hey, Little Debbie! You having an episode or what?"

She turned toward him and shook her head. Kay said, "I'm fine. I just felt a little loopy for a second. And don't call me Little Debbie, you jerk."

Taylor gave another surprised grin.

"Well, good deal," he said. "We don't need another officer coming down sick." Taylor packed the green canvas duffle bag, and then drew the strings of it tight. "I need you to walk this to three cell house. There's no need to go inside. Just pass it off at the gate," Taylor explained.

Kay picked the bag up and then slung it over her shoulder, failing at stifling a grunt. Taylor inquired if she was okay with the weight of the bag.

She tried to force a smile, and then said, "Oh yeah, just too much cheap perfume going up my nose is all. I'll be fine, lieutenant" This was a lie. She was not fine at all. Kay was trying to maintain her cool, for she was still unsettled by what she'd seen pass by the entranceway just minutes before.

Before Taylor could say anything more, she was out the door and moving down the hallway. She did not look back. She was sure that if she did, the lieutenant would have worn a queer expression of concern on his face. Kay shuffled along with the large bag on her shoulder. Finally, she stood under the dim hall light at the middle gate in what had been One Cell House. The heavy barrier slide back on its metal track to admit her. Moving along the inside wall she felt a gust of wind move past her. This was unlike the cool and somewhat fishy breeze of earlier. This gale was hot and brought along something that smelled soured.

This odor was something like the smell from an old septic tank. She felt like gagging. She bit her lower lip in an attempt to stay her sickness. Kay clenched her teeth until the urge to vomit had retreated.

"Maybe I am starting to get sick, damn it all," she muttered to herself. This she didn't need, not on her first chance to get a good look at the place, in areas she'd not been allowed to enter until now.

She continued past the middle gate. She could hear noise building from the end of the long hallway. This time it appeared to be only the normal noises of a crowded cell house. It was a bit of a relief, actually, for her to be meeting with some signs of life, made things seem more normal.

Kay arrived at the Three Cell House gate, and hit the buzzer. An older sergeant met hear and took the bag, although he eyed her with a "you lost, girl?" expression. She handed over the heavy mailbag. He nodded then walked back to his office with it.

Kay spun about on her heels to make her way back to the hallway. She did not want to go back through the area that had made her ill just minutes before. She expected another bout of unexplainable nausea, but found nothing. There was now no odor at all. Nor were there any unusual sounds, save for the echoes of her footfalls striking against the waxed concrete floor reverberating down the length of the hall.

She arrived back at the mailroom just in time to see Lieutenant Taylor returning from the count office. He was walking toward her with some fresh coffee in one hand, and a doughnut in the other. She accepted the snacks, thanking him as she did so.

"I can't have you passing out from malnutrition, now can I?" he joked.

Kay nodded her agreement, even as Taylor then continued, "I was just informed we're to do this tomorrow, as well."

Kay felt mildly puzzled. "For how long, do you think?"

The lieutenant explained that depended on how much they could get done on the dayshift, and if the mailroom officer recovered and so returned soon. Her stomach started churning again. She thought of the streaking by of the somber shade. Tasting the bitterness in her throat, she actually began to shiver a little. She had no desire to see the thing again, whatever it had been. The remainder of their shift went without incident. After work, Kay drove down the winding road away from the prison, relieved to be gone from there. The temperature was almost 80 Degrees outside of her VW. Yet, a chill gripped her she couldn't seem to shake herself free. She pulled her car to the curb in front of her home. Kay saw that her dash clock showed a quarter past 11:00 p.m.

After eating something and taking a quick shower, Kay lay down. Her dreams that night were of a small-darkened room with walls lined with nameless souls. Their eyes were black and without hope. Then there were anguished wails and stark images of torture. She felt the weight of body after body falling down upon her to the sound of steady thuds. The stench of death was overpowering. Worse, she could not struggle free.

Kay awakened then, feeling haunted. She found she was in a tight fetal position at the top right corner of her bed. The nearby fan and book lay tossed into the corners of the room, apparent victims of her night terror. Crawling off the bed, she realized she had wet the mattress.

"Oh, just lovely," she muttered to herself. Her throat was tight and sore from screaming in her sleep, or so she surmised. Her head ached, as she moved to the bottom of the bed and sat there. She finally stood up on shaky legs. Kay felt as if she had been running all night, her body ached so.

She gathered up the soiled bed linens along with her clothes.

After completing the necessary clean-up process and taking a break, she then readied herself for work. She would have preferred not to go in, but she couldn't afford to lose any pay.

The next shift went much as the previous one had, except the first part of the night passed without any otherworldly happenings of the kind she had experienced on the previous evening. Lieutenant Taylor made a good-sized dent in the logjam of mail left in the mailroom. Her break came and went. As nights at work went, the shift was had been a good one so far.

Taylor told her about his time in the military. She tried to show interest, although what he had to say made little difference to her. The dull headache she woke to earlier seemed to hang on with great tenacity. The pain, fueled by the annoying flicker of the florescent overhead light, maintained its hold on her.

Taylor seems to be a decent person, but this is not to say she was interested in him. She did not intend to be involved with anyone. This feeling went double for any possible workplace romance.

A little later, she excused herself to go to the restroom. The tea and the work coffee she'd consumed had made this trip necessary, even though there was only a little less than ten minutes until her shift ended. She rushed upstairs to the women's bathroom, intent of finding relief.

She reached the top of the stairs. She walked toward the worn, small, bathroom door. The scent of air freshener gel hung heavy in the deserted room.

She reached out for the thin cord that controlled the archaic light fixture overhead. She pulled it, causing the light to surge to yellow life with a distinctive "pinging" sound as it did so. Closing the bathroom stall door, she sat. However, she noticed the light would dim and then brighten as if the bulb were faulty. Feeling a bit unnerved by this, afraid it might fail altogether, she hurried to finish. It was then she felt a presence. There was also a strange faint sound. The noise was reminiscent of someone clearing his or her throat, but very softly.

She called out, "I'll be out in just a second." There was no reply, only a silence. The dimming of the overhead bulb occurred once again. This time, the lights took a little longer to return to full power.

Shaken, Kay called out a second time, "Ok, that's cute. I said I'll be out as fast as I can. Stop playing around." She felt sure someone was fooling with the string controlling the light.

Again, there was no answer, only that same, deep, throaty rattle. This scared her even more. Most people, under normal circumstances, would have given some sort of response to her by now. Now cautious, she pulled her feet in tight toward the toilet bowl. Kay checked the lock on the door as she stood and pulled up her uniform pants. The eerie sound trailed away as the overhead light began glowing brightly once again.

Once the sound was gone, she stepped toward the stall door. Kay stood there just inside the doorframe. She peeked through the thin crack where the door met the wall. Her eyes darted back and forth, taking in the outer bathroom area. She could feel her pulse quicken with anxiety. There had been someone there, she was sure. Kay waited for the sound of someone descending the metal staircase, or some sign of one her co-workers leaving the area.

Seeing no one, Kay opened the door and then stepped out of the stall. She kept glancing nervously around as she quickly washed her hands. Finished, she hurried out of the bathroom and then down the stairs. Glancing at her wristwatch, she could see it was five minutes after shift change. She encountered no one in the stairwell, but she didn't waste time trying to track anyone down, either. She just wanted out of the area as quickly as possible. Kay did not like this sudden-seeming trend of becoming some sort of a victim of "something."

Kay moved down the wide front concrete steps of the prison. She had her vehicle started before she had even closed the car door, such was her rush, because she had made out a human shape amongst the shadows near the staircase.

The humanoid form lifted a grotesque and misshapen arm. The dark shape beckoned her to come to it, as if it wanted her to lose herself in its ghostly embrace. She screamed as she slammed the car door shut and fled the officer parking lot. Her mind scrambled to understand what she had seen. This had appeared to be sentient entity, a shade of someone or some "thing" long since passed, or so she believed. She had read about such things. However, actually seeing something was altogether different.

Once she was well onto the main road, she pulled over onto the shoulder to collect herself. Kay sobbed into her hands. Her mind was overwhelmed. She felt so very alone and very lost by all of this.

"Why am I seeing all these things?" Kay asked herself at one point. A little recovered by this point, she rolled down the driver's side window. The soothing and familiar aroma of sweet honeysuckle carried on the light breeze, filled the interior of the car. Her mind cleared, and her composure at last returned. Wiping the tears from her cheeks, she again put the car into gear and headed back to her place.

Upon arriving home, Kay weighed her options. She was unsure as to what to do next. In the five years she had lived there, she had perhaps just a handful of conversations with her neighbors, let alone having tried developing anything resembling a friendship with them. There was a time where she could have at least leaned on her mother for whatever help she would lend. Now though, she was truly on her own, it seemed.

She no longer felt close to her mother. The years apart had done little to heal the rift that had developed between them over her divorce. Her mother's ultra right-wing outlook had not allow much room for discussion of Kay's side of the story. Kay had not even gone home for Christmas in the last year. She could not bear her mother's judgmental comments.

A dreadful feeling pierced her heart like an ice pick as she looked at her phone. "Am I so desperate as to consider doing this?" she wondered aloud. The thought of the smile of self-satisfaction on her mother's face upon hearing Kay asking for advice seemed a fate worse than death to her.

After a few minutes of contemplation, Kay decided against placing the call to her mother. Her moment of weakness had now passed.

"Buck up girl," she told herself. "This isn't helping the situation. Leaning back on the couch, she asked, "But, why me, and why now?" To this, she had no ready answer.

After about ten minutes, Kay felt herself begin to drift off into sleep. She sank into the yielding black. Kay, to her chagrin, again discovered herself again in that desolate narrow hold. Despite herself, she inched toward the area from which the torturous scene had played out just the previous night. Though the stench lingered, the room was barren. There were a few twisted chains that still hung, now empty, from heavy rings along the wall of stone.

Gone now were the trappings of her demise. The horrible twisted wall of the unquiet dead that had pressed her lungs flat was no longer present. This, along with those most terrible screams of inhuman anguish, were now gone, the room was as still as a tomb. She journeyed further still into the room.

What Kay perceived next was an unknown form in the dark shadows. The low confinement of the fetid dungeon expanded, seemed to grow. As awful as the dreaded space had been, there was a certain mock safety to its confining four walls. This place before her now seemed infinite. The possibilities for fresh horrors held within it were frightening in the extreme.

She moved about the place, taking small and hesitant steps. The noises her shoes made against the wet cobble stone floor seemed thunderous to her. Then another sound began to make itself known.

This started out as a series of intermittent dripping noises, at first distant and then gaining strength, as if coming closer. The sounds came from behind her, so Kay began to increase her pace, wanting to move away from the source. Then came a bubbling sort of cough. Now groans came from all about her. To Kay, it seemed as if whatever it was, was taunting her.

Kay, now in a panic, stumbled and fell to the hard floor. She struck her head. Stunned, she lay there, trying to recover. Her head spun when she attempted to push herself off the concrete and back to her feet. The first time was a dismal failure, as was the second. The third attempt proved to be successful.

Kay could not say if this was a side effect from the fall, but she felt distinctly more aware that whether this was real, or an illusion, she couldn't tell. She did not just hear sounds, but she could now even make out a featureless sort of figure, just a vague shape of one. The spirit, if this was in fact what she saw, looked like the one she had felt so threatened by outside the prison. The entity faded in and out of her sight. The shade, when it materialized, hovered there. A vaporous and indistinct figure. Now, as it approached her, the specter seemed to grow more solid, more real as it loomed up before her.

Kay recognized this phenomenon was the same as the one that had shot past the mailroom doorway, the gray shape with the horrible scent had returned. The closer the thing approached her, the more it gathered in on itself, became increasingly "real." Kay didn't hesitate. She ran as quickly as she could. However, she was not looking ahead of her. Kay should have been. The pain that then followed was almost exquisite in its intensity.

She held her eyes tightly shut, as if this might somehow blot out the misery Kay now felt. She felt hot, flushed, to the point she thought she was radiating heat. Kay opened her eyes, focused on the aged red brick walls of the narrow passageway. She was huddled in a corner, felt like some broken toy that had been tossed there by an angry child.

Kay felt the taste of iron in her mouth. This meant she was bleeding inside. She ran her tongue around inside her mouth, exploring. She felt like she had chipped several teeth. Then, despite the darkness in the room, Kay again beheld the luminous wraith.

The incorporeal being's form rolled and rolled, a churning vapor with only partial shape. The creature grew in size, just seemed to expand. The sickening smell of rot and death was all encompassing, along with the wet whooping of a seemingly sourceless coughing.

Kay had her back pressed into the corner as the maelstrom continued around her. Her head still throbbed from the impact, as she struggled against passing out. She could see the grey specter start to take on a more definite shape. The thing seemed to shift and flow, excess mass running off the dark center of the phantasm.

What emerged was pale and thin. The horror appeared to be a child, but with dark recesses where eyes should have been. Kay bit the back of her hand to stifle a building scream. Again, Kay tasted blood on her tongue. It was almost as if this seemed to please the phantasm. Its eyes widened. They Kay released a primal scream. Kay leapt to her feet from the couch. She swung her arms franticly about in the air, trying to strike at the phantasm she saw in her mind. Then she realized she was still home.

"Damn it all!" she shouted. "I'm sick of this crap." Kay had to take long moments to catch her breath, to calm down. She sat on the edge of the couch. After a few moments more, she pulled off her sleep shirt, which was now soaked in sweat.

Walking into the kitchen, she tossed the top into the clothes hamper. Kay's whole body ached. She no longer tasted blood, and that, at least, was a good thing. She opened the refrigerator to retrieve a cold bottle of anything she could find.

Then, she felt another presence in the room. Kay was sure the thing was right behind her.

Slowly, she turned about. Everything suddenly felt as if it happened in slow motion. Yet, everything was sharp, and felt very in focus now. Hovering there between her and the kitchenette table was the demonic ghost-child again. Gone was the hint of a loose and vague form, a mere shapeless phantasm teasing her with its possible motivation. Now the image of the thing was sharp, clear. The deep-set eyes seemed to gleam with evil intent.

Kay jumped backward, her back slamming into the countertop. Her heart thundered in her heaving chest, as she bumped along the counter's edge, trying to get away from the apparition. Stumbling, Kay fell into the one of the three kitchen chairs that sat out of the way in a kitchen corner. She gripped the top of the table there to steady herself. She needed something solid, anything to confirm what was real and what wasn't.

The entity hung there motionless. A foul stench flooded the small kitchen. This being now had its gnarled gaunt arms outstretched. Its fingertips raked across the ceiling, causing a shower of paint and plaster chips to rain down onto the floor.

Kay felt as though she would scream, but did not. She half expected to faint in fear, but could not manage this, or pray for release, either. She thought falling unconscious might well have been better to living this nightmare. Anything would be preferable to witnessing this...this...whatever it was.

The garish head bobbed at an unnatural angle. The face then putrefied, seemed to melt. Kay shrieked and then tried to cover her face with hands to block the awful vision from her sight, but she felt petrified, couldn't move. Her hands remained frozen to the table, as if of their own volition.

The apparition's thin lips twisted up into an obscene smile. The mouth then yawned opened as long streams of what appeared to be clotted blood poured out.

Kay's body reacted as if an electric current shocked her spine. Once again, desperate, she swung her arms about her, flailing them wildly in a vain attempt to strike the thing, or at least force it to leave her alone. This time, she knocked a fan against the far wall, even as she tumbled headlong to the floor.

Suddenly, it was over. Kay was home again, not lost in some terrifying vision now. She lay in a heap on the floor, the right side of her face pressed into the pale tan carpeting.

Overwrought, not even sure if she was really at last awake, Kay just lay there on the floor, unmoving for long. At last, she at last rose and shakily, sat on the edge of her bed. Kay looked about the room. All was still, silent, and undisturbed. The furnishings looked normal enough, if they reflected the reddish glow from the window of a rising sun. Other than the mess that she, herself, had caused, the place was untouched.

Even the kitchen, which in the vision had been turned into a chaotic mess by the dark apparition's crazed antics, was once again whole.

This gave Kay little comfort. The adrenaline still lingered in her blood, causing her to feel anxious and have the shakes. After putting on a fresh white top, Kay walked outside and sat on her front stoop. She let the rising sun bath her freckled face.

Once again, the question returned to her mind: *Why is this happening to me, and why now?*

After a while, Kay went back into the house. She dressed and then waited, if impatiently, for the library to open. She had decided to go ahead and make the drive to the one in the nearby town of Princeton, Kentucky. That library had a wider selection of reading material, and she needed the escape. She could drive down to the springs there, as she liked to do on occasion. She also needed to get a new fan to replace the one she had smashed to bits.

Once in Princeton, Kay told entered the library there. She told the librarian what she needed. The woman walked away, using the near silent gait that librarians often do. Soon the small woman reappeared. She held a few books.

"Here you go, miss," she said. "This is what we have on or relating to the subject." Then she asked, "What is a pretty young miss doing cooped up inside like this on such a nice day, anyway?"

Kay returned a smile, and then said, "A bit of research, I'm afraid. I'm trying to get some idea as to what exactly it is I'm actually even looking for."

The woman gave a nod. "Yes, chasing down 'old ghosts' can be trying. Would it bother you if I asked if you are from Indianapolis, by chance?"

Kay was a little taken aback. This question and the prior "ghost" comment had taken her by surprise.

Kay explained to the woman that indeed, she had been born in Indiana, at a place just a little over one hundred and fifty miles southwest of there.

The woman smiled before saying, "I thought so. The accent gave you away, hon. I had a college friend from Indy. She had that same inflection in the way she pronounced certain words."

Kay smiled, and then said, "Well you can take the girl out of the corn field, but..."

Then she gave her a wide toothy grin. Although the smile was warm, the simple gesture reminded Kay of her last night's terror.

The woman must have seen the change in Kay's gaze, because she asked, "Just what kind of ghost are you chasing, child?" to the librarian's look had now changed to one of genuine concern.

Kay was at a loss as to how to respond. What could she say? "Well, for starters, I've a creepy thing that follows me home from work? And think less Casper the Friendly Ghost, and more seventh plane of hell. Not to mention I can't sleep more than a few hours due to the nightmares dreams being so vivid and real I sometimes piss myself." No, Kay couldn't say any of that. Kay was not looking for a stay in a padded room by spouting such things to this woman.

Therefore, she opted instead just to say, "I'm just very curious about the past. A lot of craziness has happened at the penitentiary over the years, from what I understand."

The librarian leaned forward and in practically a whisper said, "I, like most people that have grown up here, have had prison guards in our families. For some of them, that place has been a hell on earth at times." Kay wanted to learn as much as she could, so she waited, hoping the woman would say more. The woman went on to explain, "There had been several escapes, riots, and multiple murders there. That's not a place for good people. It's just horrid."

Careful not to mention she was a guard there, Kay asked, "So what about a room or hollowed out place? Is there someplace at KSP with chains, maybe?"

"Hmm, sounds like the old dungeons they had in the early days. That was a veritable death sentence."

The main room of the library had stood empty, but now traffic had picked up. The woman had laid the books on an adjacent reading table. The woman smiled a slightly less toothy grin now, and went back to her work.

Kay started thumbing through the first book. The book spoke about the prison in general terms. The next did touch on a bit of folklore from the region, but nothing about the early days of the prison or any of its dark places. She opened the third book and this one seemed as if it might yield some results. She settled down to peruse its contents.

Kay saw the author had included some black and white photos, along with some stories from the prison's turbulent past. One photo was quite jarring. The photo showed a small room. The picture had faded with age, but the place was similar to that which haunted her from her night terrors.

The picture featured a low room made of rough brick. There was a flat block in the center of the room and what looked like rusted chains lying on the floor in the distance. The rush came to an end, and the elderly librarian walked back over and stood by Kay. She asked, "Well, any luck in your search?"

Kay, who had been concentrating on the book to the exclusion of all else, was startled by the woman's question. She had studied the various stories and accounts of events in the book, and felt as if she now had an idea as to just what was happening to her.

The woman, noticing her surprise, added, "I'm sorry. I surely didn't mean to startle you. I was just curious if you had found anything."

Kay explained what she had discovered in the third book. The fact there had been children locked away in the penitentiary in those days was a troubling surprise for her. Kay wondered if this was common, and if they ever had made it out of the prison alive.

The librarian said, "Life had no real value inside of that place, and this was more so for a child's life. I would imagine with the rampant outbreaks of disease that death happened a lot. It must have been pretty common."

Kay watched as the woman's face sharing a thought of a child who is sad. The woman's sympathetic look obviously demonstrated her compassion for the weak children who must have died at the penitentiary. Kay, on the other hand, was aware of the opposite. She felt she now knew the other side of that coin. For some of those children, once that fear in prison had turned to hate, such hate might well have stayed locked with them as a terrible and powerful emotion, one that followed them even into their deaths. Or perhaps, it remained behind. The rage might have grown like some terrible blackness with a sort of life of its own would grow like red plump scars that never fade away. Kay felt she knew what demons that could birth. She strongly suspected she had seen one of them up close.

Kay thanked the librarian for her help. She had all she needed now. She made her way back to Eddyville. She went to work that night. Kay found that the bulk of the mail had now been completed. All that remained to be done was the to deliver of the cell house mailbags and then to secure the mailroom.

She exited the mailroom then entered the short hallway that lead to the count office. Kay stopped and bent down at the small covered opening in the floor by the control center. She placed her hand on the now sealed door and whispered, "I'm sorry for what happened to you. It was not right, regardless of whatever you may have done. You were too young to be here, but this is not my fault. It just isn't."

Kay rose and continued about her tasks. Though she felt a presence in Three Cell House corridor, the energy stayed in the background, did not manifest as it had before. Neither did the entity attempt to make any further contact that night with her, or on any other night thereafter. The days ran weeks. Within weeks, she found the feeling of a presence had faded completely away. Kay now knew she had to be on her guard, and not just with regard to the fact there were physical dangers in a prison environment, but also those of a more paranormal nature, as well.

I, as a paranormal researcher, do believe that spirits will attempt to attach themselves to the living and often these can be negative spirits doing this. The prison is full of such lost souls, all created by depression or unstable emotions. Oppression of the living is possible in these situations. For this reason alone, I feel that if one hasn't had the proper training to protect against such eventualities, one should give the prison a wide berth. Kay had to learn this through unfortunate means, that might have had deadly consequences for her.

She, like so many people that have passed through the gloomy gates of the dark castle, has moved on to other employment. Kay now works in California. As for the wedding ring her mother had sent her, she tossed that band out as far as she could into the water in front of the prison on the day she moved away from there. With the last string cut from her ghosts, those of the prison and more personal ones, she was at last free. That doesn't mean the ghosts have left the building. They are still there, still roaming the corridors and yards at night. They still wait for the unwary at The Kentucky State Penitentiary.

CHAPTER 10

THE DEAD MAN'S LAST RIDE

Anyone either working or serving time at an institution is at a higher than average risk of encountering something dark while there, it seems. The Kentucky State Penitentiary has many items, physical devices and tools that have been used in moments of sheer terror. Many paranormal experts agree that such things, such as tools used in macabre forms of torture, or even instrument in deaths, can hold "psychic energy," much as a normal battery might. Some think the tools can also act as strange attractors and hold on to the victims' spirits once they have died. Most of these items now are in museums. However, one can still locate some of them at the prison. That is, if they know where to look.

I had a friend that was a Correctional Officer at another institution, but he had worked many years at the prison. His name was Larry. He was a solid 6'5", 300-pound powerhouse of a man. The funny thing about Larry is he was calm and reserved unless truly provoked. He was also the first person at the prison that opened up to and befriended me when I first hired there. For that, and this following story, I am in his debt.

There are dark places scattered though out the penitentiary. They are from other times and have often been forgotten. Few places have as eerie a vibe to them as the old death walk gymnasium. The old gymnasium is located by the death chamber in the belly of Three Cell House. This was where those awaiting death in the electric chair went to exercise. Once the new death walk opened in Six Cell House, the old walk and gymnasium were all but abandoned.

This area was the scene of many violent assaults and at least one murder. The gym already held a reputation for bloodshed, even by then. Some years passed before other things started to occur. Larry was a fixture on dayshift. Larry often worked various posts in the Administration building and in Three Cell House.

He had driven to work one morning through what was to develop into a severe winter storm. This day, he spent most of the day overseeing the prison-inmate yard crew in putting salt down so to prevent the walkways from icing over and causing any accidents as a result. By noon, he gave up this up as a lost cause. It was clear to him that they had done all they could in prevention. The snow was falling too heavily to try to shovel until the storm had stopped. Word came from the Captain's Office the yard was closing due to the severity of the upcoming winter storm.

The large bell in the middle of the prison yard has been rung and the inmates had all returned to their cell house for lockdown. The bell was typically used to alert of situations that can mean danger to the inmates. However, this wasn't just to protect the prison populace, but also to prevent any escape in a snowstorm. Larry saw to the lock-up. He then informed his captain there had been 15 call-ins on the evening shift already. This meant Larry needed to work overtime. The captain requested this of him, and he agreed. He didn't really mind much. Larry was unmarried, so he would have had little to do at home anyway, and that was even if he could have driven out of there, so hard was the snow falling by that point in time. This also mean some workers didn't make it to the penitentiary, although the evening shift officers that could, did manage to get to their assigned posts. Larry went to assist in Three Cell House. This wasn't unusual. Through the course of an eight-hour shift, he often worked many posts.

Fourteen-Left, better known as the cutter-walk, was his final post. He ran tunnels as a Float Officer. The tunnels were a tight fit for a big person like him. Larry had to take care not to hit his head on the hanging pipes as he made his way through them, but they had to be checked.

Many of his fellow officers, even at the time, swore the lower walks were haunted. Larry strongly doubted this. During his tenure at The Kentucky State Penitentiary, he had seen little to convince him of this fact. Larry had to admit that the tunnels did make him sometimes feel a strange sort of sensation while he was inside of them. The feeling was akin to how one would feel driving over railroad tracks. There was a funny feeling in the pit of the stomach.

Having completed the tunnel run. Larry went back to the lower cage to get his lunch. He noticed something odd, and out of place. The old coroner gurney had been freed of its mounts and now sat against the lower cage's barred door. This was unusual, as the gurney could block the exit, which was not allowed, since it could be a major hazard blocking the way in a fire emergency.

Larry only felt annoyance at what he felt sure was just an oversight. He grumbled to himself, "Who keeps messing with the gurney?" He slid the old steel cart to the back of the lower cage. The gurney's wheels emitted a piercing squeak in protest to the movement. They obviously hadn't been moved much and needed lubricating.

This done, Larry went and ate his lunch. He later went by the Count Office to get some fresh coffee.

The morning shift captain greeted him with a smile and the said: "You saved our butts today, Larry. Is there any chance after some sleep you can help out until the early-split officers show up at 5:00 a.m.?" Larry stared at the captain with a look of bewilderment and said, "Sleep, who's sleepy?" It was meant as a joke, of course.

The captain laughed. He then went on to explain that after a 16-hour shift, it was a law that Larry would have to get some sleep for safety reasons. This was fine with Larry. He finished drinking his cooling coffee and headed back to Three Cell House for a nap. Most of the better spots had other officers already bedded down in them. He grabbed some clean state blankets and pillows before heading down to the lower prison walks. On the way, Larry had the lower cage officer leave an empty cell open on Fifteen Walk for him to sleep in.

He settled down in a cell on a bunk with two thin rubber mattresses on it. Larry spent the next half an hour trying to fall asleep, but he found sleep escaped him. Something, some noise kept rattling up toward the Lower Cage Gate.

Frustrated, Larry rose and then strode to the front of the walk to find out the source of the sounds. He saw the gurney was again loose and once more up against the barred gate. Larry yelled to the cage officer once again to secure the gurney. He then returned to the cell to attempt to get the sleep that had so far evaded him.

Once more back inside the dark cell, he gathered the blankets around his head to burrow under them. This time, he managed to drift off to sleep at last. His slumber did not last long. Larry soon woke to the now familiar sound of a banging reverberating down the cell walk. He called out to the cage officer once more. This time, Larry made the officer let him inside the crash gate.

This time, Larry secured the gurney with several extra tie-downs. For good measure, he then told the officer to stop moving the gurney around. It wasn't funny. The cage officer denied even touching the old piece of equipment. The officer added that the gurney, as he put it, "is creepy, and I try to never touch the thing."

Larry, determined to get some rest, journeyed on down the walk, past the execution room to the old Death-Walk Gymnasium, to try to sleep. He felt there he might be beyond the reach of the noise, even if the guard was playing some sort of practical joke on him.

The old gymnasium interior was bathed in a dim green light. The overhead skylight, covered in a fine layer of mold on the outer window, caused this effect. Larry sat against the inside door. He stared at the 1970s-era basketball in the center of the ball court. The ball seemed to glow in the mossy green light from above.

Try as he could, Larry was unable to fall asleep again. He had the distinct impression someone was watching him. Then he heard a light rustling sound from across the dusty gymnasium floor. He turned back toward the center of the area. He could see the dilapidated basketball sitting still as a stone in the center of the stale-smelling room. Larry could hear the noise of the ball bouncing.

Not alarmed, and being practical, Larry just muttered to himself, "This is from too little sleep and too many hours of work." Looking at his watch, he saw it was 4:30 a.m.

He rolled over on his side away from the faint noise of the phantom bouncing ball. He pulled in tight against the door that led out onto the walk. With his head almost against the graying door, he could still hear the slamming noise coming from down the walk. Larry climbed to his feet. He attempted to peek out of the small center window on the hall door. The window was too dirty to see much through the glass, so he wiped a clean spot so he could peer down the walk.

He could make out the cage's barred gate. For the first time, Larry felt a flash of terror at seeing some kind of movement both in and outside of the gate. With a real trepidation, Larry eased open the gymnasium door. After going through the doorway, he locked the door behind him. He cautiously approached the gate, moving along near the darkened cell-front wall. He could hear the gurney again, as it rolled back and forth, hitting the gate with a loud thump every time. He rounded the edge of the wall to the gate to try to see who was playing games with him. He felt this had to be some sort of bad practical joke.

The air around him was now so cold he could see his breath. Larry shuddered as he walked up to the barred door. The gurney was slamming into the gate, but unaided by any anyone Larry could see. That is, there was nothing but a slight impression pressed into the padded tabletop of the gurney, as if someone invisible was sitting there.

Not a living soul was inside the lower gate room at the time, and yet, some freakish power moved the gurney. The chill he felt grew stronger around him. Larry had seen enough. He didn't hesitate. Larry raced out of Three Cell House.

He hurried to the Count Office and into see the captain. He blurted out what he had experienced. The word leapt out of his mouth as he said, "Captain I saw the gurney. I saw the thing moving like it was alive. There was not a hand on the thing. I swear to God this is the truth, so help me God." Larry was beside himself. The captain had him sit down and tried to calm him down. He waited for the captain to tell him he was seeing things, or that he must have dreamed this all.

To his surprise the captain said, "Yeah, the dead man's ride does that ever so often. That was the gurney used for moving bodies off the walk after executions. I've heard that thing banging also." Larry realized after that just how strange the prison could be.

I believe Larry encountered a ghost. This ghost seemed to be an intelligent haunt and one that was having a little fun with my friend Larry. This spirit is forever on the dead man's last ride. The spirit never wants you to forget that he has lived once and died at KSP.

CHAPTER 11

THE REPENTANT SPIRIT

A dear friend told this next occurrence to me. He died several years ago, but related this to me before his death. He had been working as a guard at the Kentucky State Penitentiary in the late 1980s. I had the fortune to have him as a friend and for that, I am thankful. He was a very earthy, practical sort of person. He was not prone to any foolishness.

He also had a strong Native American bloodline. I believe this made him more susceptible to contact from the other side under certain instances. He always seemed to have a spiritual way about him. I could read no deceit in his eyes when he told me his story. I believed what he told me to be true. Let us call him, Mike.

Mike worked segregation in Three Cell House. He was the float officer at the time events unfolded. A float officer, or "float," is a catchall position. They help with giving the regular walk officers their meal breaks, and help serve meals to the segregation inmates, among other things. Once all of this was completed, he would inspect all fire safety equipment and check pipe chases between walk cells for contraband.

The time of this event was mid-Autumn. The leaves had gone from green to various combinations of reds, oranges and yellows. Mike had finished most of his checklist of duties for the day. He knew all he had left to complete was a round on Fifteen Walk. This was the old death walk and he needed to check the cell fronts. These actions are repeated every shift.

Uniformity is the norm at the prison. Those stereotypical scenes one sees on shows on television with regard to prison routine are truer than one might think. Often, the tedium of the day-to-day routine can grind one down. That wasn't to be on that day for Mike, not on 15 Walk. There are places that hold a strange power. The one thing inmates and guards alike could agree upon was that 15 Walk was a very creepy place.

The dim half-light there often could make one feel vaguely ill, even actually sick after a while. The pale yellow bulbs seemed to possess a way to play with the shadows that resulted in a depressing atmosphere or mood to the place. They made long deep streaks of light along the waxed floors that played with one's mind. From the steps down to the death room where the electric chair stood, things always seemed somehow slightly off. The entirety of this portion of the walk always had held its own mood and this was a dire one.

Mike had just finished doing the pipe chase run. The chases are a series of long tunnels that serves as ventilation returns, as well as access to the water lines to each cell. This has also in the past served as a good point of gathering information from unwitting inmates by officers listening in as they talked to each other via the return covers.

The inmates in Three Cell House Segregation Unit often communicated by means of something known as the "kite system." Inside Three Cell House, there was no communication allowed between cells. Inmates often fashioned lengths of wrapped up paper into rods, or, as they called them, "poles." They then used these poles to slide notes and other things inside the cell tracks along the floor to each other.

The inmates also passed notes with contraband through the small openings in the covers of the returns between the cells. Contraband included such things as weapons, tobacco, and other drugs and drug-related items.

The long and narrow chases held many water and sewer pipes. These created multiple hazards and made it a dangerous and somber place to inspect.

Mike made his way up from the pipe chases toward the back opening to the exit. He had worked there several years by that point. He had made his round hundreds of times before. He had also been there for his fair share of executions. He was not a fan of this. He was not a "kill them all and let god sort them out" kind of person. He took life and death to heart. This job was his way to provide for his family. He did take pride in his job, but that is all it was for him, just a job and not a way of life. Certainly, not his way of life.

Mike returned from his break. He made his way down the stairs to Fifteen Walk. He had his Maglite ready and a plastic mirror affixed to a three-foot piece of PVC pipe. The mirror was to check the cell fronts. The cell gates slide on a track that inmates may saw to facilitate an escape. Just ask any old timer from around Eddyville about the great escape of '88. Escapes can and do happen.

He made his rounds. Mike moved from task to task and cell to cell. He knew that a lazy mistake could be dangerous there, so he always paid attention to his chores. He passed the fourth cell down and saw an inmate standing up in the cell. Mike just assumed inmate had transferred there while he had been on his break.

He paused and did a quick inspection of the fellow. Other than his clothes being old and out of date, and this was not unheard of, everything seemed normal enough. This inmate was standing and reading a Gideon bible.

Seeing him, the convict greeted him.

"Hello cap," he said. This form of salutation by inmates was a generic phrase, one common in prisons everywhere. Mike answered with a nod and a quick smile then he continued on his way. He made sure the old gurney stayed by the gate. The gurney, as others before him had learned, had the oddest habit of moving around while one would be inside the tunnels. It added no real danger beyond just creeping the hell out of someone when the creaking thing moved about.

Having completed his rounds, Mike made his way back up top. The large Motorola radio on his belt squawked to life. He was told that food was on the way from the kitchen to the cell house. It was his task also to assist with getting the inmates fed. He helped load the used trays onto the kitchen cart and it was then he realized he had never run a tray down to the inmate on Fifteen Walk.

He turned the sergeant on duty and asked, "Has the inmate on the death walk already eaten, or do I need to run him a plate?" Mike knew that sometimes miscounts on trays happened in the kitchen. Perhaps, another officer had fed the man already. Without waiting, Mike looked through the back of the chow truck for another meal.

The sergeant said, "Mike, there is no one down on that walk at the moment. The cells there are all clear. I haven't seen a soul there all day. In fact, nobody has been there in well over a month."

This comment puzzled Mike. He knew he had seen and spoken to a man in a cell on that walk just a short while ago.

Mike replied, "Well sergeant, I counted one in cell four."

The sergeant, knowing Mike to being a serious minded kind of officer, went down with him to Fifteen Walk. Mike knew with a certainty what he had seen. They arrived at cell four and looked into shadowy room. They were amazed by what they found.

The cell front was cold to the touch. The bars even had a rime of light frost on them.

They searched the cell, but the inmate just was not there. The cell wasn't occupied, and in fact was a stripped down cell, unready for any occupation. Only one item remained inside the dark cold room. In the lower part of the frosted cell bars, lay a bible. The man had vanished, but his book was still in there.

The lower cage officer opened the cell. Mike stepped inside the chilly room. Still feeling the cold, he shuddered. Mike realized his breath was clearly visible due to the low temperature. He could clearly hear the crunch of frost under foot as he moved across the floor. Little by little, the icy grip on the room lessened. Without warning, the bitter chill began to dissipate to almost nothing. This event left both he and the sergeant standing puzzled and feeling dumbfounded.

Both men were silent for several seconds. Their shared experience was very much out of the norm for both of them.

Finally, shaking his head, the supervisor said, "Damn, Mike! That was freaky. If not for that weird frost, I would had sworn you had been messing with me."

Mike exhaled at last, not realizing he'd been holding his breath. He was thankful he no longer could see his breath. Mike looked down at the small bible that lay on the floor.

He bent down and picked the copy of the scriptures up. He handed the bible to his supervisor. He could feel the blood leaving his face as he did so, for the bible was open to one certain book. This was Psalms, Passage 102:20. The time-darkened pages were both dog-eared, and well worn. Portions of the pages had been marked with a yellow highlighter. The sergeant putting on his horn-rimmed glasses read the section aloud.

He said, "To hear the groans of the prisoners, to set free those who were doomed to die." This was the only passage highlighted in the entire book.

There was another long silence between them, this time, a longer one. They were confused and ill equipped to cope with the situation. Then, by mutual agreement, both promised never to discuss what had happened in public. They had a hard enough job there without the guards and inmates thinking the cell house could be haunted. However, the thing was that they both knew what had happened. That knowledge was now their cross to bear.

When told the story, I had questioned Mike about what he thought all this had meant. Why did that particular passage of the bible pop up? Why did Mike find the book, and what in God's name did he think had produced that kind of phenomenon in the first place? The extreme drop in temperature, along with seeing a full solid manifestation of a prisoner of old was beyond anything Mike had ever seen on the hill at KSP.

Mike smiled and then he responded by saying, "I think whoever that was, this was his way of saying, 'look, even a hardened criminal like me can receive a divine pardon'. And then he was finally free."

I said to Mike, "I don't know, man. Is there a final forgiveness, one to be found here among the stone walls and iron bars of this place? Even on Death Row, is there a second chance? On the other hand, is death the end, when one is buried in a cell six feet deep?"

Mike always looked on the bright side of things. I had always admired him for that ability. I think that perhaps spirits cling to those of us with a strong center. Maybe, these sort of people ground them in some way. Mike did not like to dwell on the negative. He always wanted to push for freedom for everyone. This included the spirits of the dead, it seemed.

We had to agree his experience was an unanswerable thing. So many odd and shadowy events have happened there that at that prison, ones that have never been adequately resolved. The Kentucky State Penitentiary with its tall corridors and the high peaks and spires hid the answers to its secrets very well. What a desolate place to live and to die in, and perhaps have to go on existing in some incorporeal manner there, even after death.

CHAPTER 12

THE FURNACE ROOM

The three main buildings at Kentucky State Penitentiary were from the mid-1800s. The other structures where built later and at different times. The prison spread across the hill like a malignancy. Those buildings built in earlier, up until the mid-1900s, had seen much renovation, as well. They had to catch up with modern institutions trying to meet ACA standards. The ACA is a body that inspects various jails and prisons to see if they meet with modern standards. This all comes down to money, of course. A better score, as I understand it, means more federal money. Improvements included better accommodations such as larger cells. They combined two smaller cells so that they would meet new state guidelines. Renovators then used the remaining space for furnace rooms to help keep the inmates from freezing.

Not everyone liked these changes. This was a march of progress and some resisted change. Even so, the new layout ultimately became accepted, and the old eventually was forgotten. However, some things have a way of making people remember...

My good friend, D, told me about this next incident. This occurred in late November. His shift was in the afternoons. His post was Five-Cell House First Floor. He also was a Native American, but sported an unusually thick, dark mustache. D was a ten-year veteran of corrections. He knew the prison inside and out. He, like some of the better guards, worked there primarily to care for his family and to provide them with necessary healthcare.

He had a cool head and a quick joke most days. He understood his was a dangerous job, but even so, D never forgot to laugh some. He had seen too many guards end up dying from heart attacks due to work stress. He did not plan to be one of them. Stress was as kryptonite was to Superman for a prison guard.

Work was usually a routine shift. Every day was the same set of security procedures. Guards dealt with the same old convicts and the same "bullshit," as they put it, from the brass. However that one day, and although he did not know it, things were about to take a turn toward high strangeness for D.

The Kentucky State Penitentiary is a maximum-security prison. D knew he could expect just about anything from the place and at any time, so he was always alert. Nevertheless, there some things one cannot prepare for.

At the time of the event, most of the inmates were ironing their clothes or shaving. A few were busy washing their hair in their metal sinks. Visits were the next day and they wanted to look and smell their best for their families or girlfriends. Visits were one of the few bright points in the incarceration of most inmates. This meant a quite mellow night prior to visitation day most of the time. Most men were in high spirits (if one will pardon the expression) and attitudes were in check. The men knew that if they acted up, it meant segregation and they would have no visitation privileges the next day.

D finished checking the cell front tracks that allowed the cell doors to slide open at let-out. Security was of the utmost importance. This rang especially true for D, since he was an E-Squad member. E-Squad is the prison's tactical response unit. When a riot occurs in the institution, they have to go in hot and take the prison back.

This was not an ego thing for D to be on the squad. He knew that people could die. He cared for these people. D had always been a team player. He had also served as a mentor for many other guards.

On this occasion, all cells looked to be in good shape. This was a good start to the night. Sadly, this would change. D poured himself a strong cup of coffee and sipped at it while he ID checked all his notes from the previous shift. There had been a fight on day shift. *This was most likely a "slick check in,"* he had thought to himself. This meant an inmate owed money on gambling. Some would rather go to segregation than to take the beat down for failure to pay.

The time came for an inmate body count. This is due to the fact working inmates go to bed in the late afternoon. These men knew their roles. They were the more disciplined of the inmates and so helped keeps the hill moving along.

This type of count is to verify the presence of the inmates and any movement. Many a guard over the years had counted a homemade dummy in a cell when an escape had been in progress. Some prison movie clichés are true, it seems. D always jotted down the correct walk counts, except for today. A last minute call from a supervisor telling him to inform an inmate of a morning legal trip had made him leave the slip on his desk. Now, being conscientious, he grabbed his keys off his belt clip. D locked his office door and then went on his way.

By now, most men were in their bunks, either watching television or asleep. You would always have a few using the toilet. This was their house, though, and one just had to ride with such situations. One inmate must have been an old timer. The inmate was standing at the cell front with his ID in hand, ready for counting.

Passing the inmate's cell, D nodded in greeting. He finished this and made a beeline back to the office to call in the count.

Short of a few necessary changes now and then, one could tell what was going on in KSP by the time of day. The schedule was just like clockwork and strictly adhered to.

"One hundred and twenty-five first floor," he reported. After a short pause the voice on the other end of the line said, "That is a negative, officer. Recount please."

D placed the old-style green receiver back in the cradle of the rotary phone. He was a little upset and not a little annoyed. Such things did not happen often. Moreover, D was damned thorough, but somehow, he must have missed something. Off he went to repeat the process. This count was the same, and with the same exact results.

The old convict was still ready with his ID in hand up at the cell front, just as before. D glanced at the old man but kept on counting. He didn't want anything to screw up his count for a second time. He slid the old tarnished key back into the office lock. Turning the key, he could hear the tumblers falling into place like some ancient tomb trap door on Indiana Jones. He then called in to report the same number. He was sure it must have been a mistake on their end and not on his part at this point.

He reached the control center and told them his latest count.

The voice replied, "I'm sorry D, that's still off. I'll send up the yard supervisor."

D knew he had counted every soul on that floor.

He thought, *Okay, once is possible, but twice on a miscount? Something is up.* The old yard sergeant arrived. He huffed after walking up the several flights of stair to the first floor.

"Okay, D, I was listening to the UK [the University of Kentucky] game in the count office. What's up?" the Sergeant asked with mild indignation in his voice. In western Kentucky, UK sports events were less a sport and more a religious requirement. One did not play with a man's money, family, or UK game-watching.

D told him what happened.

The old sergeant said, "Well, let's do this then, and hope to God this isn't an escape. I don't want to have to wake the warden with that kind of news."

D nodded in total agreement. Most wardens came in limited types:

1. Do not bother me, whoever you are.

2. My door is always, but you had better not bother me.

3. This was the last. He was the "no-waves guy." This meant "No waves. I do not like waves!" The current warden was a number three, and very much a "no-waves guy." This meant one had better make sure that before one called him, that it was truly a life or death issue.

This time, D and the yard sergeant went and did the bed book count together. This showed exactly who was in what cells. This type of count is an ID count.

The walk count went off without a hitch. The same held for B and C. as well. D Walk came up the right count.

"Wait, where was the old guy?" D said. "I don't remember seeing him on this last count."

"What old guy?" the sergeant asked. The count had gone well. The elder sergeant did not understand why his officer found fault with it.

D felt suddenly queasy in his stomach.

"The old guy, the one in the middle of D Walk?" D questioned. Both he and the sergeant then walked back up the dim inmate walk. Both had their flashlights on and flooded the cell with their beams. What D saw made him take a step back.

The cell was now a heater cell. It had been a heater cell for decades. The sergeant then asked D, "This is where you saw a man, here in this converted cell? Are you sure?" The sergeant studied the cell once more. He knew what he had seen that night. He felt reasonably sure had hadn't gone insane...

"I don't play on stuff like this, bubba. The inmate was there." D said, as he looked at the sergeant. They both examined the cell front again. They were looking for any sign of any tampering. There was nothing unusual. The sergeant, half-chewing his lip continued the count moving to Echo Walk. The count was right this time.

D sat in his office with the sergeant. D said, "I don't care if you think I've gone nuts. He was there. The man even had his ID ready."

The supervisor looked at D, who patiently waited for some sign of acceptance of his statement. The sergeant looked away. After a minute of staring out the office window, he said, "In the mid-nineteen hundreds, there was an old timer. He was a real old-school convict. When he was mocked by another inmate that he was losing his cell due to the renovations, he stabbed the other man to death at let-out."

D sat there, half convinced the sergeant was just messing with him. D replied, "But, I saw this man tonight! How is that possible?"

The sergeant shrugged. "The convict always stood at his cell front holding his ID waiting to be taking to segregation. He saved face; that was all he had." Both men fell silent. Neither knew what to say in the incident report. These reports document any unusual events in the prison.

"I saw a ghost. Jesus Christ," D exclaimed.

The sergeant replied, "There is no way that is going to fly with the warden." Both D and the sergeant agreed this was a simple "miscount." D told me he never again did a count without a count slip in hand. He did not tell me this story until years after he left KSP.

He still had family working in corrections then, and did not wish to bring any hardship to his family. D said, "I've been all across the country and I've seen many things. I have to admit that this was new." He never brought the encounter up after that. I suppose he thought things were better left alone in that regard.

I often wondered to myself: Did D witness a ghost? A recurring spectral loop of a soul confined to a fixed point in time waiting to die. Or was this an intelligent haunt? How did he cope with having undergone such a strange phenomenon? Did he think I could help him come to grips with this somehow? Well, D did just manage to cope with that until his health got to the point where he had to bow out of prison work. Life at the Kentucky State Penitentiary is always difficult, and no one walks away without having been affected in some way.

CHAPTER 13

WALK OF THE CONDEMNED

Death Row has the name "the walk of the condemned" for a reason. That walk is a collection of America's worst offenders, as well as some victims of unfortunate happenstance. For some of us, Death Row is about final justice and a final sense of closure. This is not so for those sentenced. Inmates see this as a place of nightmares and regret. The Death Walk is a place of contemplation for murderers, and, ultimately, is their last stop.

The last few decades, those Death Row inmates lived in the cells down on Fifteen Walk in Three Cell House as they neared their date of termination. At the end of that narrow and solemn walk stood the death room. This was a thirteen-foot-square room with a window on one side. This viewing room was there for the families of the victim and state officials. Just inside the steel-reinforced locked door and to the left was where they kept the electric chair. This malevolent collaboration of wood and steel was called "Old Sparky." The use of the chair fell out of fashion in many states. However, "Old Sparky" still has a home at the Kentucky State Penitentiary.

I, and other paranormal investigators, believe that certain objects or areas involved in death have the ability to harbor the negative energy of the condemned. They carry the last fleeting influence of cognitive thought of someone cooking alive from the inside out. I research this sort of phenomena. I do this, not just out of some morbid fascination I have, but also better to understand the possibility of the paranormal in the first place.

A prison death chamber is a place that most choose to avoid for obvious reasons, although some are carried away by a dark fascination for such things. I know firsthand the way that particular walk can gravely affect a person. This effect is even more powerful if one is sensitive by nature.

The next incident I'll discuss is about my first week at the Kentucky State Penitentiary. Making the transition from a job in the public sector to one at the penitentiary is a strange and somewhat schizophrenic one in some ways for many people. The odds of a new hire making it to the end of the first year are slim at best. The instructors teach a lot about rules of conduct and the letter of the law, but they often fail to tell the toil this sort of environment takes on one's soul.

I, along with the rest of the new hires, was on a tour of the institution one day. For me, this was wonderful to be able to be at last see inside the dark gothic architecture. I had only seen the penitentiary from the street as a young boy. The "newbies" were impressed, and more than a little intimidated by all they saw. The prison is unlike anything most small town people have ever seen.

Some of them did not return to work after that day. When asked, they could not explain why they felt that way about the prison. It seems that for many of them, everything in their gut just told them to run and stay far away from the place. The old officers though they were "weak." Not me. I think maybe they were the smarter of us. I've heard someone say the prison was not a place for decent people. I would even go one step further. The prison was a place of death, pure and simple. KSP is only fit for the dead, and those awaiting death.

We had made the first rounds on the prison yard. The tour consisted of the basic stops around the penitentiary. We first visited the inmate kitchen. The kitchen in the early 1930s was where a bloody siege had taken place. You could still see bullet holes in the yellowed dinning walls next to the large steel industrial steamers, ones used to prepare most of the meals there. The kitchen battle ended after much blood had been spilled.

There was then the shower house. Lastly, the laundry and the walking track made up a large section of the yard tour. These places made many uneasy. There are many blind spots in them, ones well away from any hope of immediate help if trouble broke out. Moreover, they could feel the eyes of prisoners on them, and could hear the cat calls from out the cell house windows.

I saw this all served as a very motivating reminder that one is not meant to feel welcome there. The hostility of the inmates was clear and direct. The anger was as real as a homemade knife to put to one's throat and this did happen, on occasion, to guards.

All of these locations had seen their fair share of violent acts. Hell, there was not a five-foot-square area on that hill that had not seen blood spilled. I heard there is a weapon about every thirty feet there. I later found that estimate to be conservative. I had learned in confidence that most fearsome inmates kept a weapon within feet of their cells at all times. Luckily, for me, I always kept a good relationship with the inmates. I treated them as men. They responded well to this approach.

We then came down to a series of locked gates to the outside door of Three Cell House. This reinforced metal door with a small safety window inserted in it immediately let one know that this is where all the action was to be found. This was where most people think the worst of the worst spent much of their sentence.

The average inmate there might range from an altercation with another inmate or staff member though to being guilty inside of much worse deeds. Most guards looking to prove themselves in combat yearned to work there. This was, after all, at times a modern battle arena. Now we were there on the tour; it was a very busy place, as it was mealtime. We were there right as the lunch trays had been gathered and returned to the kitchen in a small, battery-powered and boxed-in golf cart named "Blinky."

We made rounds on the various tiered walks. The walk officers escorted us along these. The cells were small and you could see the effects of solitary confinement on the men in them. Some yelled and threatened while others sat shredding paper into small strips. Some rocked on their bunks. At times, we learned that a handful of inmates went as far as to harm themselves or to defecate and rub their bowel movement all over themselves. Needless to say, this wasn't a pleasant area of the prison.

I wondered to myself, *Was it rage or madness that I saw in their eyes? Could it be possible this was due to the effects of the evil that is said to inhabit these walls?* I still can't give you a definite answer on this. Working from what I know of my time there, though, I will relate what I felt inside of Three Cell House.

We marched down the walk. Rows of cell doors visibly bounced from kicks of the inmates as we passed. Jeers and a cacophony of wails from them continued as we made our way off the walks through the manually controlled gate. The cage officer secured the key box and we all regrouped. We then continued with the tour in Three Cell House.

We walked down the metal grated stairs to the concrete main floor of the cell house. Everyone took a moment to gather their wits about them once more, tried to mentally regroup after what they had just seen. I studied the others, gauging who I thought would be the first to go.

The administrative tour guide paused and said, "Well, you've seen most of segregation, anything else you would like to do before the tour is done?"

Several of the newbies expressed a desire to visit the Death Hold Walk. This walk was located downstairs on the old Fifteen Walk corridor. This came as no surprise to the administrator and so he was happy to oblige. I was pleased to hear this, as well. I've heard so many claims of the paranormal and oddities about the walk. I was ready to get to experience this firsthand.

I am sure that this will seem ghoulish to some. However, this is human nature. When people pass a horrific automobile accident, they have to slow down and take a good look. It's these "rubberneckers" who cause the resulting traffic jams. This behavior seems to be part of our makeup. Some make jokes about dark things. This behavior is a shield used by anyone that deals with life and death situations. Most people know it as "gallows humor."

With the ever-changing montage of death and suffering that played out there, this is something needed at the Kentucky State Penitentiary, this ability somehow to cope with such things. We began the walk down the narrow stairway to Fifteen Walk. I do not know why it was so gloomy down there, but it was. The best way I can find to describe that walk was that it made me feel rather ill.

On that walk, one first comes down some gray metal steps. One then moves past a blackened corridor of old pipe chases. These were added some years after the original building was completed. The walk itself is narrow and has low ceilings due to the added ductwork. The lighting remains at a miserable minimum.

The light fixtures have the dull, thick-glass style of protective light covers over all the bulbs. And it is a weakened yellowed light that is cast from overhead, and which then reflects off the faded cream tiles of the walls and floor. A single cell walk runs a span of maybe twenty-five feet. The two inch by eighteen inch security windows on the outer facing wall give no real reprieve from the melancholy this sort of lighting induced.

The walk commanded an immediate and very somber response from me. The cells were small and basic. There was not much in the way of getting your mind off just why you were there, I suppose. This was the running chute up to the slaughterhouse of the execution chamber. To make matters worse, there was also the buzzing drone of those lights and the ventilation system's incessant and monotonous sound. They sounded very much like one of those big bug zappers to me, just waiting for its prey.

I stepped out onto the walk. The air around me was tense and oppressive. I felt a great weight as I passed each cell front. There were remnants of great misery there. If you have ever been inside of a pig farm or a meat processing plant, you will know what I mean, the feeling one gets. KSP is very much like that, a factory for institutionalized death, plain and simple.

A cool dead wall was what meets the gaze of those inmates who stared out of their prison cells. No cells were opposite their own. The builders, it seems, did not wish to afford the condemned the luxury of another face to look at or to keep them company. There also kept the cells free of anything that the prisoner could use as a device of escape. This was also to reduce the chances of suicide.

Once we reached the end of the walk, there was a guarded room. This was the death room. Old Sparky inhabited this place. I say "inhabited" because I see Sparky as more than a mere tool of demise. That chair was more than a macabre mascot of the prison. This was the soul of the "beast"—the penitentiary—in so many ways.

Some inmates have gone to the chair with much bravado. Some remained stoic, while other shook and collapsed along the way. The old emotions to me were palatable, as if still residing there like some palpable residue. Perhaps this was due to me being somewhat empathic. Regardless of the reason, the longer

I strode that walk, the more resolute I was in the belief in the existence of the paranormal.

Entering the room, the first thing one realizes is the size of the place. This is a ten-by-ten-foot square. It was such a meager space to try to contain the death of a man, I felt. Everything in its construction was designed to put the chair in the center of attention. The fullness of the unease of being in that place was heavy upon me. I did my best at shielding my concerns from my tour guides. I tried to remain resolute. I steadied my mind as best I could.

Everyone received a chance to touch or to sit in Sparky. Some did while others refused. I, after some thought, sat in that seat where so many before had "ridden the lighting," as the old timers used to say. This was a twisted rite of passage at Kentucky State Penitentiary. I must confess that it was morbid curiosity, as much as from respect for the dead, that I chose to sit there.

So I sat down into the killing chair. I wondered what the dying must have thought about and felt while waiting for the switch to be thrown. They would be listening to the clicking of the clock counting down until midnight. The sound of families lamenting their coming death, even as the reporters scribbled on their pads to get the story in before the other one next to him would have been heard in the background. The prisoner knew life would go on without him.

As if by instinct, I gripped the wooden arms of the chair. My arms tensed and grew rigid against the wood. I pictured my chest swell with one last great breath. I felt strange then. I experienced a type of tunnel vision. I noticed things seemed to take on an odd and disconnected quality.

One macabre discovery was I found there were hundreds of deep fingernail impressions burnt into the underside of the chair arm. This, it seemed, was the last act of many a dying man. This was the last refusal to submit to this claim on them by the state. I soon rose and left the chair. It was too much. I had seen and felt enough.

Then I looked on while the others took their turns in the death seat. Some pretended as if they were frying. As I watched these unpleasant antics, I raised my hand to scratch my nose. This was when I realized that my hands had an unpleasant scent to them. The seat held a foul odor. They could not get the charred smell of death off the armrests. The stench was a part of the chair, as much as the straps or the leather seat, and was imbued with the odor of death.

We left the death room and headed back up toward the front of the walk. I could sense some kind of lingering presence nearby. This was like a sickening pressure, or, rather, oppression. I felt like as if someone was behind me, as if some school bully ridding right up on your back and breathing down on your neck, one lurking and daring you to turn around, but of course you never do.

The closer I edged toward the walk front, the more intense the sensation had become. I let the newbies go on up ahead of me. I fell back with the administration tour guide. I looked at him before saying anything. He was an older man with a round pleasant face and red tuffs of curly hair encircling the top of his head. He had worked there for years as a correctional officer before gaining his current position.

I asked him "So how do you deal with the pressure down here?"

He looked at me a moment and then apparently realized I did not mean the job stress. He gave a slight laugh and then said, "Oh, so you can feel that too, huh? That never really goes away. You just make a sort of peace with it."

We reached the end of the walk and the pressure was stronger. I felt nauseous. His revelation that it was real and not just my overactive imagination hadn't helped. I started moving up those clanging metal stairs and then noticed the feeling began to subside. We moved swiftly across the main floor, and then on towards the outer exit. We reached the door to the outside and now the strange pressure was all but gone.

One may wonder what had I experienced. Was it real? I thought so, and so did that older guard. Perhaps the sensation was an imprint of all the fear, anxiety, and stress in the fevered minds of dead men walking. This event was my first formal introduction to the Kentucky State Penitentiary's "shadows." These lingering souls, or the residue of them, had never received a reprieve or a release date. It is my and other paranormal researchers' belief that they still remain there to this day.

As a researcher, I have also wondered if there are some places on this Earth that get soaked with enough blood that this causes them to evolve a taste for it. The death walk is, in my opinion, just such a hungry place. I will add this for those with a bit of a ghoulish nature; yes, my hands carried that horrible scent for days. This was regardless of whatever I put on them to try to get rid of it, or however much I washed them.

CHAPTER 14

OLD RED

The thing most people who have never been inside KSP fail to understand is the prison has a subculture all its own. This is one with unspoken rules of conduct and social mores. This is a city unto itself. The prison is more than a place to secure inmates. The inmates are more than just slack-jawed, steely-eyed loners looking to terrorize weaker convicts. The Kentucky State Penitentiary was a community, perhaps like most in that it was dysfunctional.

The prison manages all makes and models of people convicted and sentenced to serve for acts that society deems "bad." Hollywood likes to glamorize the young tough person with perfect hair handing it out to the guards in a fun fight. The reality is, more often than not, most come for short stays of five to nineteen years. Not everyone gets out still having a heartbeat, though. Some live and then die there. As a paranormal researcher, I believe some never leave, not even in spirit.

A former guard that moved up and out of The Kentucky State Penitentiary and into then into higher government told me this paranormal account he experienced. For the correctional officer's name, I'll use Q. I had known Q since he was a child. He had been a marching band kid. I've three at home and, yes, it gets loud there, but we love it. Q was well schooled, and quick-witted. I was surprised when I heard he was coming to work at the prison.

Q, like most new guards, was cross-trained on various posts. This made them capable of running a variety of positions. The thing about places such as Maggie's was they had turnover like mad. As previously mentioned, most new officers never finish the first month. The older guards ran gambling pools on who of the new "fish" would cave in and quit first.

Q proved them wrong. With time, he began to gain the trust of the older guards. One day, there had been a call in on morning shift. By this point in time, Q has a reputation as a solid officer. He volunteered to go work the post.

That post was the infirmary. The hospital was located at the far end of the prison next to Six Cell House, which houses Death Row. The current hospital replaced the original infirmary that was burnt down in a riot there years before. Actually, the infirmary was less a hospital and more of a clinic. It was a clinic in what amounted to being in the middle a war zone, but this was all they had. Complete with heavy metal doors and barbered wire, the infirmary was every inch about maintaining security and control of the patients. This facility was to be the stage for a major play in psychological terror, as it turned out...

Q made the walk out toward the infirmary. Springtime meant the steady fall of rain in this region of Kentucky. The storms seemed ceaseless, permeated one's very bones with chill, as the water tapped against the concrete on the walking track. This distance separated him from the infirmary and the hopes of a dry evening and a hot cup of coffee.

The light drizzle enveloped Q. At last, he made his way up the walk to the gate. He moved into the secured foyer of the front of the building.

The evening shift officer heard the sound of Q arriving outside. He made his way from behind the inmate-crafted oaken desk next to the cage that barred the front metal door. The officer greeted Q and gave him a quick update on the one inmate housed in room two. The officer then gave him the keys. He then left.

Q walked around the cage and placed his small igloo cooler holding his lunch down on the desktop. He noticed the other guard had left a real mess all over the desk. The trash was full and a still smoldering soda can filled with cigarette butts sat on the floor next to the chair by the desk.

This place smells like stale piss and low ambition, Q thought. The prison seemed to hire the dregs of humanity more often than not. Q knew it was something he couldn't change, so he just had to accept it. He sighed and cleaned up the mess. He did not have time to gripe, in any case. He had much to do. Q had to run a security round and get a count called in.

The layout of the infirmary was a circle of inner rooms used mainly for inmates. The outer rooms were staff and doctor offices. Somber and utilitarian in nature, as was the norm in most prison architecture, they weren't exactly cheery in their look.

Q began his round. He was responsible for checking all locks and rooms. He was also responsible for counting fire extinguishers and medical supplies. This was hard because of the dim lighting the night settings of the overhead lights provided. He made his way around the hall onto the inmate wing. Their medical rooms had large observation windows made from security glass. The "cutters," as some of the inmates were known, stayed in isolation.

He was no fool. Q knew well enough to approach any cell with care. One approaches an isolation cell with the absolute highest discretion. Q had to "see flesh and movement" to call in a solid count. He moved forward toward a dusky room's window. Q peered into the cell front to look in on the inmate.

The convict, named King, sat very still. His knees were pulled up to his chest as he sat on the stone bunk. King was very odd. There was no other way to put it. To see him on a busy street, one might not even have noticed him. King was a man of slight build and a dull expression. He was as a simple silent shadow.

Q studied King for a few seconds.

He appears fine. Well, fine for King, Q thought. One sees many damaged people locked up, ones damaged in varying ways, some mentally, some physically, and some both. Some did not belong there. King was one of those. He was a criminal, but was also borderline mentally handicapped. He had a weakness for heroin and for stabbing young co-eds on the dark streets of Louisville, Kentucky. Somehow, King had ended up at KSP. He spent most of his time between protective custody and the segregation unit.

Q rose up to continue his round. He could hear King's muttering trail off, as he turned the corner at the far end of the wing. He checked the small kitchenette area. He was thankful he had brought coffee. The coffee pot was bone dry. Everything else seemed in its place. Q hoped this would be a cakewalk post. He called his count into the Captain's office. Signal 14, or count clear, by the count officer soon played over the walkie-talkie.

His round done, Q sat down at the desk and updated his logbook.

"Christ, how many farts did that evening-shift guy pump into this chair?" he asked himself, for there was a distinct odor still.

The next few hours came and went. King's gibberish, along with a cricket somewhere inside the building, were the only sounds to be heard. The nurses came down from the station located in the Administration Building to check King's vitals. They gave him his meds and then walked back to the front office where they shared gossip.

Then, they gathered their things and left to return to the nurse's station for early pill call. Personally, I cannot understand why in God's name anyone would spend years in medical school and spend thousands of dollars on their education just to work in a prison. That always seemed odd to me. The nurses left and the infirmary was silent at that point. Beyond the gibberish in King's cell and the chirping cricket, the halls were like a silent tomb.

The time was a bit past 3:00 a.m. when Q looked up at the camera monitors showing the wings. The lights on the inmate walk were dimming, as if they were somehow losing power. They pulsed, as well. Then they seemed to steady, or nearly so.

At this point, Q could now hear King whimpering loudly enough to drown out the cricket. On his next round as Q walked beneath the overhead light above King's cell, the lights began dimming again. King had again ramped up his incoherent talk and cackling. Q drew his flashlight from his belt holster. He tapped the Maglight against the light fixture.

The blow against the florescent light was direct and effective. The tubes flickered and flashed back to full brightness.

"Thank God for old engineers," Q said aloud. King lifted the sheet from his face. Q noticed he looked both frightened and relieved all at once.

Now, King's rant was back, along with the clicking cricket who hid in a wall or under a desk somewhere. The clicking started to unnerve Q a bit, but he could not explain why this was so.

Q settled back in at his desk. He noticed the rain had all but ceased falling.

Thank God for small favors, Q thought. The first hues of pre-dawn painted the skies in the east. Due to the storm, the sky was otherwise a sickly yellow-green color. A sound had begun to creep up from off in the back storeroom, one Q hadn't been consciously aware of at first. The sound was not from a cricket. He was sure of this. The noise was metallic sounding. This sort of thing was just not common at around four in the morning. Q knew there was no staff there to be making any such type of noise. The sound carried an eerie tone to it.

There was no help for it. Q again made his way down the hall and rounded the corner on the medical wing.

King was lying on his bunk, seminude, and rocking back and forth. The cell held a strong scent of defecation. Q surmised that King must have stripped down for what smelled like one hell of a bowel movement. King's legs and arms showed pockmarks. They looked like scars from a fire many years ago. Q shook his head. Who knew what the poor man might have gone through.

Q decided King was all right. He continued moving toward the storage room. On the way there, he heard King muttering, "Red knows. Sure as the rain falls, Red knows."

Reaching the rear hallway, Q turned toward the storage area. The sound was still there. Something behind that faded office door was rapping out its two-tap clanking noise.

The short hall was dark. After lights out, there was no real need to keep lights on for just stored brooms and soap packs. He unlocked the door and pushed it open. Q could see nothing beyond the threshold of pitch-black doorway. He fumbled for the light switch. Upon flicking it on, the row of bulbs exploded in a flash of blinding-bright, blue light.

The shattered bulbs hissed as the shards hit the concrete floor like tiny pieces of brittle ice. Then only the dim red filament of the bulb remained before it faded away to darkness.

"This is nice to see freaking state dollars hard at work," Q said, under his breath, as he coughed from the scent of burnt tungsten wire that still hung in the air.

He turned on the flashlight. A steady beam of light illuminated the glass-covered floor. He saw nothing there that somehow could have struck the light fixture. Q gave an audible sigh of relief. He was not one for walking blind in on strange noises.

Using his flashlight, Q began to scan left to right as he started down the old storage hall. The light found only old metal doors with ancient metal locks and hinges. Once he realized nothing was out of place, he turned toward the front of the hall where the pale florescent lighting still glowed on the walls.

He had almost made his way past the corner there when he again heard the grind of metal on metal from behind him. His throat tightened. Q knew no one was supposed to be in the hall; that is, no one except him. He pivoted on his heels. His body flexed, his fists fixed for any threat. He still saw no one. His eyes darted from door to door. About midway, they came to a rest on something odd.

Down the hall on the right, his flashlight illuminated a lock. The thing was rising and then slamming down. The lock struck with a loud clanging sound against the door. Over and over, this occurred.

Amazed, Q wondered, *Am I really seeing this? How is this even possible?* Watching this all play out, he exclaimed, "No-no-no..."

Q stood there, as if mesmerized, as he later put it. He tried to rationalize what he was seeing. The air was still, yet the heavy lock moved unaided. Q then backed up and out of the hall. His flashlight blinked and then faded to black. He was in complete darkness, unable to make out what might come for him.

He leaned against the outer wall of the hall. The sound, thankfully, had abruptly stopped.

What the hell did just I see? He wondered. Was this a play of light or... Q didn't wish to ponder the matter further. Instead, he wiped his brow and then turned up and into the well lit medical hall. He moved well away from the storage area. As he did so, he felt some measure of calm return to him.

He went into the kitchenette area. He turned on the faucet and splashed his face and neck with cool water.

He dried himself with the rough paper sheets that were the prison equivalent to toilet tissue. One will not find these babies in a Hilton.

I had best get my last rounds and count done, he thought. *Focus on the job. Then get the hell out of this place.* "Nope, do not care for this place at all," he said aloud to himself.

Q made his next few rounds. Nothing was out of the ordinary. Even King had calmed down a bit. He just droned on with a dull mumble. Q smoked his last cigarette. He was fine. He was going home soon. He picked up his trash, and put away his lunch bag and his now empty thermos.

He made his way past the storage hall. He braced for something off occurring there again. Not a click or a clang this time. He went past the kitchenette toward King's cell. Q had an odd feeling then, sort of a mild unease. He paused a second by the doorway to the kitchen area. He was aware of something in the hallway.

A sound emanated from behind him, directly behind him. The noise was the sound of someone sucking his teeth at full volume and this seemed inches from Q's ear. It was if someone was trying to clean old meat from between their teeth.

He now heard a click-clop sound, as well, like a pair of old-style boots, the kind with wooden heels. What was worse, this sounded as if it was coming after him.

Q quickened his pace up past King's cell. This time, King was right up to the slot at the entrance. His eyes were wide and darted left and right. Apparently, he had heard the noise, too.

"Red knows. Sure as the rain, he knows," he said. King was wearing a wide garish grin on his simple face.

"Shut the hell up, King," Q pleaded. He didn't need this crap on top of whatever the thing was that was playing with him.

Q regained his nerve enough to turn to face down whatever goblin was making his night a living hell. He drew all the courage he could muster as he braced himself for what he might see. The sound was louder and closer. Then, it was still closer, until the phantom clicking came from right before him. Q saw nothing there. He only could hear the click-clop of boots where there were none.

Q now done with this madness, said, "Enough. I'm here doing my job. Don't mess with me and I won't bug you. Have we got a deal?"

"Oh, he knows, boss. He knows…" King continued in a slight whimper. The disembodied sound now changed to a cacophony of clicks, pops, and hisses and came right up to his face. The reek of foul old tobacco stink assailed his nostrils. This hung in Q's throat like soured tobacco spit. This sensation caused Q to back up against the hallway wall. He felt crushed by the entity's noxious presence. The force, with a chilling motion, moved though him and then on past. His reaction was immediate. Q thought he might puke. He smelled smoke, and felt the heat of a fire. Q would have sworn he had heard people screaming. It was all he could do not to pass out. He stood there, frozen to the spot. The roaring sounds and the visions faded.

As he came back to himself, he heard King gently sob, "Red knows, and now you know too. You know too…" Q could see the tears well up in King's eyes as his voice trailed off.

Q had once heard of a young inmate. He could have been no more than eighteen. The young man had been working in the old infirmary. He was then beaten and raped by a group of stronger inmates. The boy tried to fight, but they had beaten him badly, to the point of his blacking out. Fearing that they had killed him, they set fire to the old infirmary. They left the boy to burn to death.

Their crime would have died with him, if not for an old trustee. An old, round-faced Irishman most called Red ran into the burning building. Red soaked a blanket in water and wrapped this around the fallen boy. The trustee snatched the boy up and carried him to safety. Although the boy received severe burns, he survived.

Red, however, was not so lucky. He died from complications from the smoke inhalation a week later.

Q said with amazement, "That was you. You were that kid in the fire. The one you keep calling Red is the trustee who saved you."

King smiled and said, "Old Red kept me safe. He still does."

Q heard the door buzzer alarm that was his relief. He left the infirmary and never told another soul other than me of what happened that shift. I've asked around some of the older guards about any strange history connected to this sort of event. This phenomenon has happened to several guards, apparently, and at various times at the new infirmary. Those old, clicking, wooden boots and the locks moving and slamming have startled many working at the hospital.

I understand this sort of thing is not for the faint of heart and can be hard to believe. People want to be logical in their assumptions. However, if you can entertain the concept of a life after death, then perhaps this story had meaning for you. It did for me.

CHAPTER 15

THE POTTER'S FIELD HORROR

Some may wonder: What happens to the convicted dead? What hell awaits such sons of perdition? Kentucky State Penitentiary is the prison now famous for the heinous crimes carried out by many of the prison's infamous inhabitants. At times, KSP has been a veritable killing field. Just walking outside along the cold walls of fortified stone can fill most hearts with a primal fear.

The conditions do not matter if you have an inmate doing a life sentence for a murder, or one is murdered by the state. Even when one meets with death by order of the commonwealth, in time something must be done with the body. Most inmates have families that claim them. Others donate their corpses to science. Then there were those who died without family or financial resources of any kind.

This experience happened in the spot where indigent inmates sometimes went to their final rest. It is a place where the friendless dead, unwanted by anyone, are placed. This, too, is where "something else" awaits, a creature cloaked in rumor and superstition. It is said that dark things happen in the dense forests of Lyon County. That "things" wait for the brave or the foolish to step into their world.

A potter's field is an unmarked graveyard reserved for the poorest and the cast-offs of any given society. The one at The Kentucky State Penitentiary remains littered with the unlamented and forgotten graves of convicts. This place is set deep in the woods located behind the prison. The land has no trespassing signs and is unmaintained and unacknowledged by any who might care. I've spoken to many locals as to an exact location. Most either cannot agree, or will not talk about it at all. Some even say the place moves around to differing spots in the ancient wood.

All of this fuels the mystique of the now legendary KSP potter's field. Without any clear markers for the dead, they receive no recognition. It is said their souls cannot pass over in peace. This hypothesis is plausible to someone who has done extensive paranormal research, as I have. There are only stories though, ones without evidence to back them. The truth awaits those that wish to dig deeper.

This experience came to me from the son of a former officer from The Kentucky State Penitentiary. In the case of many small towns, most people grow up, work, and die within twenty miles of home in this area. My friend was not of that mold. He and his family wanted more for him. That is why he wanted to become a doctor and they supported him in this calling.

Aiden was a first year medical student attending nearby Murray State University. He was a bright, athletic, young man. His family moved from the small town of Eddyville to Murray when he was just eight years old. He was also an avid hiker and day camper. He would explore some of the local forests during the occasional visit back to his homeland, for he still had some friends and relatives in the area.

During his fall break from his studies, he visited aunts and uncles. He enjoyed catching up with family and friends at these times. Striding through the small town square, Aiden often marveled at how little had changed since his last visit. Even as nice as everyone had been on each visit, he felt like time stood still here. He again found his mind calling him to roam the lonely forest trails there once again.

Aiden met up with his cousin, Riley. He had invited Aiden into his spacious lake house. The home had a huge wraparound deck with an ornate stone walled circular fireplace. The deck also boasted an impressive view of the prison across the water. Most of Aiden's Eddyville relations still had strong ties to the penitentiary. The conversation soon turned to hunting stories and old wives' tales.

Riley's girlfriend, Amy, and her friend, Shae, had brought out a small serving cart with mugs and hot cider, as well as a platter of ginger and almond cookies. Soon the stoked fire was giving off heat, even as the sun dissolved into a brilliant sunset just beyond the silhouette of the brooding penitentiary.

Aiden told the group of his love of parkour, or free running.

"Murray has many great places to run," he said, "but I miss the trails here most of all." He knew most of the county woods very well. However, Aiden had heard legends of odd things rumored to live in the deeper woods, although Aiden had never felt scared there. He and Riley were both big fans of day hiking and camping. The girls, however, preferred camping only so long as they were in a camper, or at least a cozy three-room tent with access to Wi-Fi. They just did not share the boys' deep connection to nature, or at least, to roughing it.

Aiden loved the trails he had often run on in Eddyville. He hungered for a new challenge. They all discussed areas in the LBL National Park. The topic of the old bluffs in nearby Princeton, Kentucky came up. This area had at one time been an encampment for a tribe of Native Americans. All of these were great choices for hiking. Aiden brought up one that was local and most stood out for him.

"What about the old prison graveyard?" he asked. "Was that the place your dad talked about being back up in the woods?"

Riley nodded agreement. Both of the boys had grown up hearing stories about Vinegar Hill, as the area was called.

Shae laughed with slight unease, and then asked, "Why in God's name would you want to visit a bunch of old convicts' bones?"

"Men," Amy said. "Ha-ha!" When the girls had retreated to the house once more, Aiden seized the opportunity to bring up the potter's field topic once more.

"You know Riley," he said, "we could pack up a little gear and make this a night hike, a boys' night out."

"Well, brother, I know very little about that patch of woods. I'm not saying no, but it is uncharted territory."

"That's the whole reason why I want to do this, Riley. What do you say, tomorrow night?"

Riley sighed, and then nodded, before saying, "That sounds like a first-class bad plan. But I say let's do this." They then went inside. Across the water, the lights of the KSP were still visible.

At about 2:00 a.m., Aiden and Shae pulled out from Riley's driveway onto the county road. They traveled over a series of narrow county roads.

After dropping her off at her parents' home, Aiden sped off toward his cousin's home. Aiden liked that his car now held the lingering scent of Shae's perfume. He was half-lost in a song on the radio when something darted across in front of his headlights, and clipped the top of his car before rolling over his roof.

"Shit," he exclaimed, as he slammed on the brakes. The car fishtailed though the loose gravel. He tried to turn into the slide to correct this issue and so the car came to rest in a cloud of rock dust, but now sitting sideways on the road. Aiden sat there a minute, stunned. He was sweating and unsure what just had happened.

He put on his flashers and shoved the car door open. Aiden inspected the vehicle, and saw where something had struck the top of the windshield. He looked up the road to verify that there was nobody coming. He walked to the back of the car to try to see what he had hit. The pulsing flashers coupled with the still present road dust mingled to produce an alien, if not hellish, atmosphere.

Moving his hand to diminish the glare, he could see a small figure. This dark mass lay just to one side of the road. He approached the heap. He could make out what appeared to be blood-splattered, owl feathers scattered about the road near the twisted lifeless body. Yet, there was something more.

His eyes, now having grown accustomed to the dim light, made out a new shape lurking just past the body. There were full red eyes gleaming in the blackness. The thing emitted a low, throaty growl as it advanced. Aiden backed away, almost falling against the trunk of the car in the process. For a moment, the beast seemed to study Aiden. Then the creature latched onto the bird and melted back into the darkness, vanishing.

His mouth was dry from fear. He returned to the car and climbed into it. His mind raced as he engaged the starter. He had driven some distance before the rush of adrenaline had subsided.

"What in the hell was that?" he asked himself. "Maybe it was a wild dog of some kind." Alternatively, was it a wolf, perhaps? No, not likely, because a wolf hadn't been spotted in the region for years. Yet, he had seen something.

* * *

Riley looked up from his plate and said, "Holy crap, the dead hath risen," as Aiden came into the dining room for breakfast the next morning.

Aiden stole a quick bite of the egg-coated venison that sat on a platter before him on the table. "I had a bit of an event last night," he said. "I hit an animal on the way back here." Aiden then went on to recount the events of what had happened after he and

Shae had left their house. They finished their meal. Aiden and Riley stepped outside to inspect the damage to the car.

Riley walked around the car then said, "Well, whatever the creature was, it didn't seem to have done any real damage, just bloodied the car up." There was dried blood at the top of the window that trailed off over the roof. Aiden inspected the damage, as well.

He said, "This looks like some kind of bird. I think it was an owl. I didn't have much time to see what snatched the thing up, though." Riley went on to speculate the animal might have been a coyote or a feral dog.

Aiden shrugged. "Yeah," he said, "maybe."

Aiden had seen a lot of wildlife on wooded trails over the years. He knew what a coyote and a wild dog looked like. This had been something altogether different. Coyotes, unless they are ravenous or ill, avoid direct contact with man. Neither coyotes nor dogs shared the sheer size of the monstrosity that had almost caused him to wreck on that old county road the night before.

They had a quick lunch. It was agreed that none of what Aiden had seen the previous night would get back to Shae. They all decided it would only worry her. Moreover, Aiden knew he had nothing validate his sighting, to prove what he thought he had seen. He realized the fact was that the thing on the road could have been anything, just distorted looking in the dim red glow of the taillights of the car, and lurking as it had been in the dark woods. Aiden knows there were many odd things said to be in the woods. This was the first time, though, that he had encountered something of such a nature.

The next morning, Aiden and Riley began the plan for the night expedition. This was necessary, for one did not enter the woods without proper preparation, nor without a proper mind-set. A night run would end quickly, and not well, if one tumbled down a ravine due to poor lighting. Both of them were earnest in wanting to think this run though for all such possibilities. They did some brainstorming. The boys came up with a decent list of necessities.

They started gathering the gear they deemed necessary for the hike. They had taken care to check everything thoroughly. One didn't want to be out miles into the woods only to discover they had left a much-needed piece of gear at home.

Riley's dad, Jim, stopped by to say hello. Jim was a son of a correctional officer and he had learned many secrets about the penitentiary through him.

The three walked down to the water's edge where Jim learnt of their intent to have a night's outing in the woods.

Jim stared into the cold waters of the lake as he said, "When they first built the penitentiary, they had to clear the lands around it. The march of progress stops for no one, it seems. There was a town here where you now see the lake, old Eddyville. The families were forced to pack what they could, and leave their homes to face the great flood without them. The government gave them no choice in the matter. There are parts of those homes still beneath the waters, waiting. You have to be careful. Things lay in wait. They sleep, waiting."

This cryptic speech left the boys with a decided chill. Jim turned and looked at them, and then said, "Ha-ha, I'm just shitting you boys. There nothing up in those hills, but ticks and a hard night's sleep. All the same, do try to be careful, kids. Beware the 'haints,' ha-ha."

Aiden and Riley walked back up the hill. Aiden said, in a sour tone of voice, "That Uncle Jim, what a kidder."

There was about two and a half hours left until sunset. The sky had taken on a blue-grey cast. Aiden then loaded the last of the gear in his backpack. Riley used the little time left to spend with Amy. Shae was stuck at home with a migraine. She had texted Aiden she was excited about their first official date on the morrow. He had read this after a quick attempt at a nap. He had tried to sleep, although he was too excited about the hike to get any real rest, it seemed.

He was able to type out a quick, "me too," before Riley came rapping on his bedroom door. The time had come to leave. They hopped in Riley's S-10 truck and sped off down the driveway. Riley glanced over to Aiden. He said, "With any luck, we won't see any Bigfoot or swamp monsters out tonight."

Aiden's stomach tightened at this. "I hope the same," Aiden murmured.

Anyone knowledgeable knew the inmate graveyard could be reached by going through the prison gun range. The prison had stakes in the ground to mark the location of the unclaimed bodies. However, this route could lead to an arrest by the state police. The range was prison property. They didn't allow non-state employees on the property.

The two drove past the winding road leading to the prison. Riley knew the field farther down the road, less than a mile or so. They turned off onto the water authority road and finally reached the start of an old dirt road.

Riley said, "See, I told you. This is supposed to lead to the field and the trail goes to the graveyard."

They turned down onto the abandoned rutted trail. The path wound down alongside what appears to have been a spillover, which was now clogged by a beaver dam. A dense canopy of foliage hid the open sky. The years of nature's unchecked reclamation had allowed the roadsides to become a wall of tall weeds and brambles. Their progress slowed to a veritable crawl.

Their truck came to an abrupt halt.

Riley said, "Well damn." A series of large trees had fallen across the road and blocked the narrow passageway. This ended any further continuation with the S-10. They knew they would have to hike in from there. One could hear the crunch of the twisted green wall of vines echo down the hollow.

In a facetious tone, Aiden said, "If I see a headless horseman, you're on your own."

"If I see him, I'm tripping you and then running."

Seeing the remaining pale light through the trees weakening, they decided to pick up their pace. Both grabbed their backpacks from the truck bed and then started down the ever-darkening trail.

They began pushing their way into the deep woods. They wound around through hills and trenches. In these wild areas, losing one's bearing in unfamiliar woods is common. This seemed to be what was happening to them now. The waning light dimmed further. The sky took on a ruddy hue as the sun set. They knew walking blind under such conditions could result in harm to them. At this point, the boys at last broke through into small cleared spot. This was a rough, fifteen-foot circle just uphill from the small creek they had been following.

The spot was less than a few months old. A local hunting group, they assumed, used it. The area was close enough to the road to seek help in the case of an emergency, and was still well into the region of prime hunting tracks. They had noticed several deer ruts, as well as some places where the tall grasses lay flat from something big having been there in the recent past.

A fog had begun to appear near the water's edge. The mist now obscured all but a few yards ahead of them. The only illumination came from the LED lanterns Riley pulled from his backpack.

Aiden asked, "So how far off are we now? Can we make it there with the small lights we have with us?" Riley, he knew, hadn't taken the fog as a possibility when preparing for the trip.

Riley said, "This is pretty late in the season for this sort of fog to roll in. We might be stuck here until it clears. Our lights won't help much against this, so we better prepare for camping here overnight." Aiden had to agree. There was no way in hell he wanted to get lost or hurt by running blind and falling off into a gully. They busied themselves with setting up camp.

Aiden made a small, Navajo, in-ground fire pit while Riley set up the two-man pup tent. The fire was to keep them warm and ward off animals. However, they wanted to keep the fire small, because they did not want to attract attention. They were most probably now on prison land. They set the tent up so they could face the path. They would see or hear anything or anyone that might happen upon them this way. This also afforded them the ability to meet whatever threat might occur that way head on, instead of being blindsided.

The fog continued its oppressive march on the pitch black woods, creeping along like a thing alive. The only sounds were the trickle of water on the rocks below the campsite. The two huddled together by the fire, waiting for the fog to pass.

At this point, Aiden noticed something odd. There were no animal sounds. There were no birds to be seen. In fact, they did not see anything common to the woods there in the way of normal nightlife.

Riley noticed this, as well.

"Damn, this is weird," he said. "There isn't as much as a fox out making noise. That's kind of creepy."

"Maybe the weather has them all bedded down somewhere."

Riley, lifted his eyes up from the fire he had been tending to gaze out into the dense swirling mist.

"Yeah," he said. "Maybe, but one thing is for sure, something has got them spooked, and big time."

A few hours more passed. The boys begin finally dozed off, huddled together at the front of the small tent. The mist gave way to a steady rain. The fire pit had cooled to pale embers. The few sounds to be heard were the patter of rain against the Mylar pop-up roof of the tent, along with the babbling of the filling creek.

It was then, as Aiden later informed me, that Riley frantically shook him awake.

While Aiden had slept, his cousin had come to and had realized the fire was going out. He had slipped out to feed the fire. Riley had let Aiden sleep. He had crouched down, coaxing the flames. This was when Riley had begun to sense something was different, off.

He looked around, but seeing nothing, had then crawled back into the tent. Checking his watch, Riley saw the face read nearly 4:00 a.m. Glancing out of the tent, he began to make out movement and some noise coming from just beyond the clearing of trees. Riley listened for any further sounds coming from the rain and still dense fog.

His breathing quickened when the noise returned, and this time was closer toward the small tent. He still couldn't see anything, but not wanting to be caught unprepared, Riley fumbled around inside his pack for his knife.

Meanwhile, the sounds had faded yet again. The rain had worsened, and this made it harder to hear much beyond the incessant pounding against the now trembling tent. He looked back from glancing at Aiden just in time to see a figure pass between the fire and the tent. He sprang back from the doorway and then rushed to wake Aiden.

"Aiden, wake up man. There's something right outside the tent. Come on! I'm not playing around."

Aiden, now awakened asked, "What the hell, man? Are you trying to spook me or something?" Aiden saw the tent rocking in the wind and thought it was maybe a tree limb. As Aiden's senses came to him he became aware of something indeed was there.

They crouched there for several minutes. The fire, now rained-out, gave a final sputter and then belched a cloud of gray smoke. Both boys had drawn their knives. Any thoughts of sleep were gone. The first subtle tones of dawn were coming to the sky when they unzipped their tent and peered out. They could see nothing wrong. They moved with caution as they exited their shelter.

Seeing no tracks, they continued their walk down the now washed-out trail. The fog hung on the path like Spanish moss. Pushing aside the undergrowth, they made their way down the twisting path. They quickened their pace. Both wanted to get to the graveyard by dawn. As they moved up an embankment, they began to hear noises behind them on the path, in an area they had just traversed. The darkness prevented them from making out if anything was there.

Something behind them emitted a prolonged growl. This reverberated down the path and, being so loud, even seemed to vibrate their chests. They heard something coming swiftly up the path towards them. Whatever the thing was, it seemed large and heavy by the thunderous galloping noise that came through the shifting fog. The boys both broke into a run. They rushed down the narrow path, barely able to stay on their feet, due to the slick mud.

The noises moved closer and became a succession of long howls and moans. This animal was not a coyote or some farmer's sheep dog out for an early morning stroll, this much was certain. The thing had a seeming intent and focus. They abandoned their backpacks and made a mad scramble up the hill.

Mounting the hilltop, Aiden stole a glance back over his right shoulder. Breaking though the tree line behind them was a hulking mass. Though obscured by uprooted bushes and fresh fog, they could see its fearsome outline. This dark terror was on four legs, yet stood almost as tall as a man. The beast's head rose, shifting left then right, scanning to maintain their scent. Steam came from its mouth. The hellish thing's teeth were exposed. They glistened in the predawn glow. The beast saw them and emitted a loud scream of rage.

They watched the horror advance toward them. Riley gasped and recoiled at the sight of the fiend. The eyes showed a clear malevolence. The beast charged them, forcing them to continue their retreat up the ravine.

Aiden pushed Riley to move to do this, because he stood frozen in front of him. He had to shake Riley to get him to respond. They sprinted, half-falling up the steep incline in their haste. They lost their knives in the ascent. The shadowy looking thing was almost on top of them by this point in time.

Clawing their way up the mossy hill, they pushed their way through rotting leaves and wet earth. The ghoulish creature snapped long bared teeth and bellowed a hair-raising wail.

Having just made the top of the hill, Riley screamed out, "The thing has me. Oh shit, it has me!" Aiden looked back. He could see in the growing daylight that the terrible thing had Riley's boot in a nightmarish claw. Riley's face was a twisted mask of fear.

Aiden screamed, "Fight, Goddamn it. Kick him! Kick him!"

Aiden pulled hard on his cousin's arm as Riley, using his free foot, stomped manically on the creature to attempt to free himself from the smoldering fiend.

"Get the hell off of me!" Riley shouted, and gave another determined kick. At last, Riley's foot came free. The rain must have made the slick boot slide out more easily, acting as a natural lubricant. Aiden, along with Riley, fled over the hilltop backward. They tumbled down the slope on the other side.

Over a series of stones and roots, they continued to tumble. Their eyes filled with dirt, which temporarily blinded them. Then, they landed hard on the forest floor at the base of the hill. It left them winded and dazed.

On unsteady arms, they pushed themselves up to stand. The boys strained to see the supernatural hell that had hunted them. Wiping their eyes clear, they could see the thing stood atop the hill, above the tree line. They looked behind them and saw only a thirty-foot rock face blocking their only means of escape. They knew now they had nowhere else to run. The hellish shadow-beast paced back and forth, as if plotting what to do next. They boys, still shaken and not comprehending what they were experiencing, looked about in a panic for a weapon. Aiden found a shoe-sized stone lying in a patch of weeds that encircled them.

Aiden and Riley stood there together with their stones at the ready. Having nowhere to run, their lone choice was to stand their ground, despite the pitiful weapons they held. They shifted their weight from leg to leg, anxious, anticipating a charge from the creature. Trails of a pitch-black, smoke-like substance streaked from the form. The eyes still glowed with malevolence.

After another minute, it became clear to the two of them that the horror was not coming down the slope after them.

Riley whispered to Aiden, "What does that thing want? Why isn't it coming after us?"

Aiden had no answer for this. They waited as the dawn's light began to finally stream over the hilltop.

The full rays of the morning sun shone down now, and a bright light through the trees illuminated the whole of the hillside. The creature reacted immediately to the strengthening light. The monster shrank from it, though it still refused to flee. The thing now looked like a partial shadow, one that was in the shape of a beast. The horror moved in a disjointed way, seeming to move jerkily, acquiring new positions without actually having moved smoothly to them, as if it was in this world only part of the time. The light shone through the smoldering form. Then, the thing convulsed in a thrashing display of violence. With a high-pitched screech, the spirit beast, or whatever it was, seemed to evaporate.

Aiden later told me they had sat there for a long time, stunned. They would not move until the sun was strong overhead.

Both men were in a form of shock and needed several minutes to collect themselves, to consider their situation. They wanted to make sure things were safe enough to walk out of there.

Riley who was still holding onto his stone, called out to Aiden, "I'll be damned. We're here. We've made our way here. Look at the stones."

Aiden looked down at the old stones lying about them. At his feet were shoddily made headstones. He looked all around. They were everywhere among the rotted wooden markers. The two had found the potter's field. They, by blind luck or otherwise, had stumbled upon Vinegar Hill.

After returning to Murray State University, Aiden began researching what they had seen that night. He was trying to make some sense out of what he and his cousin had experienced that frightful evening. In his studying of the experience, he found many similar accounts. Several legends spoke of wild spirits of the woods.

As best as he could guess, the spirit creature was some sort of hellhound. This was a type of demonic ghost beast. Many cultures believe these inhuman entities haunt the outsides of graveyards. They are vicious and are always ready to kill. There have been stories of them for millennia, it seems, and from various cultures.

Aiden had learned that since the old graveyard was still sacred ground, the shadow could not stand upon the sanctified soil, or, for that matter, withstand the full light of day.

This whole ordeal shifted Aiden's view of the world around him. I had to wonder, *How would one feel if their childhood boogiemen were proven to be real to them?* Too many cultures have claimed to see them for such things to all be fantasy, I feel. And where did the idea of such things come from? It seemed unlikely that unconnected cultures, over millennia, had just invented them.

A final note; Aiden never walked through those particular woods again. The Kentucky State Penitentiary, he felt, could keep its secrets. He wanted nothing more to do with them. He would still take day hikes in other places, although never at night, and never in Eddyville. The fact was Aiden had become a changed man. No one could live through what he and Riley had and not feel altered.

CHAPTER 16

THE PRISON CATS

Oh yes, there are verifiable ghosts of a sort at the Kentucky State Penitentiary. You can see some there almost every day. They come and go at all hours of the day. Their deep, hungry eyes are always watching you. They lurk in the shadows with their needle-sharp teeth and those long, talon-like claws that will shred a person asunder, if they so choose.

They linger, slinking about in dank dark corner, as well as under the sleeping inmates' beds at night. They move about and are always hunting their prey. The prison administration ignores them and the inmates care for, and even revere them. What are these strange denizens of the hill, one may ask?

They are the prison cats. Inmates cannot legally have pets at the institution, but believe me, they are there by the dozens. There is even a policy for the cats to be spayed or neutered every few months by a visiting veterinarian. This was the prison's attempt to keep from having a runaway feline population explosion. Such an event would lead to disease, as well as other problems.

I remember back when I had been posted as the front gate officer on day shift. Many weekends, I worked the front gate. I would process the local veterinarian into the prison at various times.

The one question one must oneself is: why and how this came about, to be as it is today? The answer is we are, after all, a strange culture. We display a dualistic nature sometimes to the point of schizophrenia. Our society loves horror and violence on the one hand. On the other, we love sappy black and white Christmas movies. Those hundreds of videos of kittens playing pianos on the Internet do not get a million likes for no reason...

For all of our shortcomings, we hold cats in high esteem. One has just to go and wander the crowded aisles at any grocery or convenience store. A towering display somewhere of our abject devotion to cats will usually be found. These are in the form of seemingly hundreds of variations of gourmet cat food on shelves there. All of them are adorned with happy smiling kitties, most with wagging tongues.

This is not such a strange thing in and of itself. The strong emotional attachment we humans seem to have towards felines has been with us as a race since the time of the Egyptians. This went beyond basic admiration to full religious fervor. The Egyptian goddess of music and joy, among other things, is Bastet. She was a feline deity who could be either cat or human at will.

The worshipping of Bastet first began around thirty-five hundred BCE. It was not until closer to nine hundred and thirty BCE that all of Egypt embraced her and so began the institutionalized worship of this most ancient of Egyptian goddesses. This daughter of Ra the sun god ever protected her father from Apep, also known as Apophis. This great serpent god was her father's nemesis.

Early Egyptian society believed the cat held natural supernatural powers. They felt cats could serve as a conduit to the spirit world, as well.

"How does all this dovetail into a paranormal prison story?" one might ask. Well, we will get to that shortly.

First, it should be understood that inmates, on average, and more often than not, come from underprivileged homes. This goes hand in hand with broken homes and lower school test scores. This, in turn, can lead to those children dropping out of school. This, over several generations, results in an increasingly uneducated and superstitious population, and one with a statistically much higher likelihood of committing criminal activity.

The subculture that is the Kentucky State Penitentiary has, within the towering fences and crumbling edifice, several races and religious beliefs. There are various Christian sects. There are also Native American faiths, as well as druids, and even witches. The prison affords religious inmates a meeting place to practice their services.

They even have Satanists. Most of those last devotees I had dealt with seemed laid back. Many inmates fought in court to be able to practice their faith so long as this did not compromise the safety and security of the institution. Security is the bottom line in most decisions at KSP.

One inmate was a worshiper of Bastet, and loved his cats. They were his children. This story is something of an odd morality tale. Even inside a walled-up world one composed of murderers, rapists and thieves, everybody knows that nobody touches the cats. Those who did dare to did not stick around very long.

I was a young guard at The Kentucky State Penitentiary at the time. I was lucky enough to have been taught by some very seasoned supervisors. Those men looked as if they could handle themselves in even the direst of circumstances. The other guards respected them, as did the inmates. They would not play games and would go full on "assholes and elbows," as the rather colorful phrase went, if necessary.

I use to refer in jest to them all as hard tack guards. Hard tack was a type of provision used as rations during the Civil War and later. This was a thin cracker or biscuit made of a simple flour water and salt mixture. They were hard as nails and twice as salty. Those men were like that, hard and salty, because they had seen truly horrific scenes play out in the belly of the beast known as KSP.

They gave me some very helpful advice. These were insightful life lessons I've never forgotten. The big three pieces of advice goes as follows:

Number one—one never falsifies the count. It is the most basic job and yet the most important thing a guard can do at the prison.

Number two—if you mess around and screw up, just admit it happened. There is nothing worse than being a liar in regards to matters of state security.

Number three—This is the most important, and it is never to harm a prison cat if possible. Being that I am mellow person, and not so inclined toward ritualistic animal sacrifice, this seemed a simple request. The seasoned guards seemed to appreciate my respect of these simple rules, as well as my compliance to their sage advice.

Most of the rules in play at the penitentiary are reactive. The feline guardianship policy was a reaction to something that had occurred earlier.

The protection extended to the cats stemmed from more than a humanitarian concern for the animals' welfare. Harming a cat is a serious cultural taboo in the penitentiary. Prison taboos are something most people outside of jail would never even consider to be an issue.

Bryden was "a troll," as my father used to say. He was a brutish type. Not a redneck, as a redneck can hunt and pull off some useful tasks. No, Bryden was more of a racist bully who could only survive in a workplace like the penitentiary, because he was lazy, except when taunting people.

He was not impressive in any way, and neither did he hold any sort of a real intellect. He was a narrow-minded man-child. Bryden hated homosexuals, minorities, and anything that was beyond his dim arc of interest or perspective. He and the few likeminded cronies that did subscribe to his brand of bullying would spend their days running about and terrorizing the prison populace like some band of slobbering ogres. Some men are born mean and some are born dumb. Bryden was born both. I If anybody deserved a Spartan-style kick in the behind from karma, that would be Bryden. The season of the event was the start of true winter. This was a freezing mid-December day, 1980. The thick cover of trees that crowded the prison grounds were now barren and looked more like sticks shoved into the ground.

The wind was from the north and howled long and hard. The temperature had been dropping throughout the morning, and now was hovering just above freezing.

"Well, this is going to be a suck job out here tonight. Well, ain't it, Jerry?" Bryden asked, as he pushed his considerable bulk into the prison yard office, and then over toward the wall heater.

The yard supervisor, Sergeant Jim Leveave, or as Bryden called him, Jerry, just to be annoying, bristled from the shot of cold air that assailed him from the still partially opened door.

"Close that dang door," he ordered. "And don't track up this floor. I had just mopped in here, ya idiot." The irritated supervisor went to reorganizing the scattered pile of papers that he had sorted mere moments ago.

Looking up, Jerry, with a high-pitched sigh in his thick Boston accent, asked, "Aw Jesus H. Christ, Bryden. How did you end up getting out on the yard?" Jerry had no time for Bryden, or his roughneck tactics. Nor did he need Bryden's foul, Skoal-smelling breath on his watch. Jerry thought Bryden was about as useless a man that he had ever had the misfortune to encounter.

Bryden rubbed his fat mitts in front of the blower of the small electric heater.

Jerry again posed the question of the hulking officer, but this time more forcefully. This time, he asked, "So what are you doing out of Three Cell House, then?" Jerry waited for some sort of answer.

Bryden stood there as if transfixed for a moment, but he didn't reply.

Jerry gave him a hard probing look now. His eyes were bright under those fiery brows. He was a thin man, maybe all of five feet three inches, but no more. He was also a former military officer. He was the dependable kind. However, this also meant he had no patience with brutish hicks like Bryden.

Bryden now leaned against the desk until his beer gut lay fully bare upon the corner of the top of it. Then Bryden cocked his oversized head to one side, and gave a sly smile.

"Must just be my lucky day, I guess, ole Jer," he drawled. "I get lucky every once in a while, you know."

Jerry then gave a quick, disgusting-sounding chuckle. The plucky supervisor kicked both of his feet up hard onto the desk, just narrowly missed smashing Bryden's grubby fingers in the process. Bryden jerked back. Losing his footing, he almost tumbled backward into the wall behind him. This sent the sheets tacked up on the yellowing board flying in all directions and scattering on the floor.

Bryden's eyes were wide now. His mean-natured smirk now reduced to a mere half-smile. His cheeks flushed blood red. He did not like being the victim for a change, it seemed. Bryden said nothing, but just hovered there, silent. Looking sheepish, he paused while spinning the mental wheels inside his head. It was clear to anyone who watched that Bryden wasn't used to this sort of treatment, and so had no immediate defense, or response, at hand. One will find it is often like this with most bullies. They rely wholly on the frailty of other people.

Bryden was not a deep thinker. He was much too busy making inmates and coworkers lives miserable. Darkness seemed to feed on him, or he on it. It was hard to tell. This is why he loved his job, though: the darkness.

Bryden apparently decided to play this all off with a quick laugh. He was smart enough, at least, to know when and where to pick his battles. He quickly regained his redneck composure. He spat a long stream of coffee colored liquid into the tattered wastebasket at the end of the desk. Bryden wiped the remaining spittle from his chin with the back of his hand and then rubbed it against his work pants.

"Good thing that I'm quick like a fox," Bryden said.

Jerry, instead of immediately responding, wadded up some paper napkins and tossed them over the tobacco spit now pooling atop the refuse in the basket. Jerry then gave him a stern look.

Bryden said, "Had a last minute call in. They pulled me out of Three Cell House to help my good old buddy, lieutenant Jer, out."

Hearing, "Lieutenant Jer," set the supervisor's teeth on edge. Bryden used a paper napkin to blow his nose, then wadding it up, he tossed it toward the wastebasket. He missed his mark by a wide margin. The paper wad flew in an ark that sailed by the now-bristling supervisor.

Bryden grinned then said, "Hmm, guess I ain't gonna be getting that schor-lo-ship," in his best redneck shtick.

"Get the hell out of here, Bryden," Jerry commanded. "Go and check the fences. And I want your round to take a while." His face was now red.

Bryden stood there a moment with an angry expression on his face, and then, without speaking, followed his orders and left the office.

Jerry muttered to himself in disgust, "Pffft, schor-lo-ship, are you kidding me?"

Outside, Bryden shuffled down the stone incline that winds down from the yard office toward the paved walking track. The chill night air meeting the still warm, blacktopped walking track had caused a thick low wall of fog.

The moonless sky was clear of clouds and a handful of stars showed beyond the light pollution. The night was silent and eerie beyond the shuffling sounds Bryden's feet made. The only other noise was the faint humming of the out-of–date, overhead security lights which broke the silence.

He moved along the rough-cut wall of stone. He ventured past the low brambles and ankle-breaker rocks that could trip the unwary, and that lay strewn about in the nearby gully. He then breached the P.I. wall that separates the main yard and the prison industries section of the institution. P.I. is nestled in the lower back section of the place.

I heard on more than one occasion that correctional officers would at times hear sounds of machinery operating in off-hours in prison industries. There was even talk of the occasional scream from the far back fence of the area. I have not been able to authenticate this, however. These sounds, along with reports of phantom lights moving along the yard gate leading down to prison industries, do make this an odd place to be. This is especially so at night.

Bryden, on the other hand, liked visiting this section of the penitentiary at night. The back wall was free of a good portion of the noise of the main yard. The stillness made him think of a western ghost town. He was a big fan of westerns. The big man thought he could have been a real big deal back then. Cracking heads and squeaking beds. That was what his limited intelligence held as being the true nature of the Old West. Limited smarts and a stout back were like gold then, or so he wrongly thought.

Bryden had made his way across the sloping hillside in P.I. when he came across one of the cardboard cathouses put there by the inmates for their pets. He hated cats. Bryden always had experience an instant, strong, and visceral disdain of them. Judging by the noises emanating from the cardboard box, it sounded as if there were a few cats inside.

"Fee-fi-fo-fum," he muttered low to himself, acting is he were some kind of vengeful giant from a child's bedtime story. He brought his right foot down hard against the first three boxes. Several cats scattered thought the high grasses in a chorus of hisses and screams.

Most of them found their way free of his clumsy feet in this terrible attempt at animal abuse. He fumbled with and then freed his Maglite from his belt. Bryden depressed the rubber "on" switch. The flashlight sent a burst of harsh light into the bank of fresh fog. Bryden had to cover his eyes from the flash. The air around him shone, glowing with a sphere of foggy luminescence.

His vision improved and then grew accustomed to the light change. He was able to make out the hint of fresh blood on the now dilapidated cathouses. There were also sprays of blood on the tall blades of grass that framed the edges of the uneven sidewalk. A thin red streak ran along the seam-leathered toe, of his boots.

Wiping his boot clean, Bryden continued on his way. He could see the fading metal fences, as well as the interior wall through the mist. The gates and locks all looked fine. He then started making his way up the hilltop and through its resident halo of mist. This made Bryden quicken his pace, for the fog made him feel a little uneasy now. This, along with the mix of foul odors from the slop dock nearby, only added to the unpleasantness for him.

Bryden soon arrived at the outer yard door. He entered the Administration Building. He came through the final outer gate. He could see Lieutenant Jerry studying him from a distance. Jerry hooked his thumb over his shoulder toward the front gate. He did this in a "get on to work" hand gesture. He was busy operating the switchboard from inside the control center. Bryden motioned he was going to get a cup of coffee first.

Jerry, too busy to protest beyond mouthing the word, "Moron," went on about his business.

This amused Bryden to no end. He rounded the corner toward the count office door still wearing his goofy grin.

He had a fresh hot cup of coffee in tow. Bryden checked out the keys to one of the Ford Crown Victoria interceptors from the Control Center. The Control Center was run by a newbie who was still trying to remember what keys went to which vehicle. Meanwhile, Jerry had taken off to make rounds outside Three Cell House. Bryden shot the kid a quick "bird" and then went on his merry way.

The breeze was coming in with gusto from off the Cumberland River. The windstorm pushed hard and for a moment made him lose his footing. The gale blew down into his collar, chilling his exposed back.

Continuing down the well-lit front entrance steps, Bryden caught sight of more blood, presumably from the night's earlier "festivities," now dried black and flaking off his pant leg. He looked down at the spatter and smiled.

As he walked, he turned the key chain around to remember which car he was to use. He turned his head then, the better to hear something. Off in the distance, maybe at a nearby home, he thought he had heard cats calling out. His eyes narrowed.

Nasty cats. Next time, I will take my sweet time and get all of y'all, he thought.

Jerry called him on his radio, and asked, "Are you about done out there? I need you back up on the hill to help relieve officers for break as soon as you can get there."

Bryden replied, "That is a ten-four, Lieutenant, just as quick as I finish up this perimeter check." After he disconnected the call, Bryden murmured an unsavory epithet to describe Jerry.

It was almost 9:30 now. The fog had relented just in time for the first snow of the season to start falling. Bryden had made the full circle on the perimeter road outside the prison by this point.

Bryden headed for the front steps. He could see Jerry standing beside the desk, just inside the foyer of the Administration Building. Jerry waved over his shoulder to the control center to open the front gate, so he could process Bryden back into the penitentiary.

"So you ran out for a pizza, or what? You took a long enough time out there," Jerry grumbled, as he passed the last of Bryden's gear through the metal detector.

Bryden said, "Damn snow made things take longer. You can't blame me for that. Safety first, boss."

Jerry sent him to relieve the Six Cell House walks office for a break.

Bryden again made the trip across the unforgiving prison hilltop. This trek was now more arduous, due to the quarter-sized flakes that blanketed his path. His footsteps made light crunching sounds as his boots left muddy prints in the inch or so of freshly fallen snow. His mind went back to the sickening crunch of cardboard and the streaks of steaming red. He had enjoyed that.

Meanwhile, Jerry checked the next shift roster. Sitting and watching the heavy snowfall, he grimaced at the radio's weather report. The expected continued snow accumulation through the night could become an issue. In such case, this often leads to a bout of the "blue flu," meaning people would call in, saying they couldn't make it into work.

Bryden made his way into the cell house. He accomplished his round through Six Cell House. Most of the inmates were in their bunks with blankets pulled up to their eyes. By contrast, one lone convict sat cross-legged, with his tattooed back to the cell front. He seemed to be lost deep in some sort of prayer. He chanted softly.

Bryden walked on past him. He approached the other illuminated cell that lay further down toward the end of the walk. The cell had a short, middle-aged man inside. He sported a slightly scruffy salt-and-pepper beard. He stood there with his fingers interlaced over his pronounced paunch. The inmate was still as a statue. He just watched Bryden in silence.

It was then Bryden felt as if he had been pushed into the air. It seemed as if he floated about, locked inside of a small, highly pressurized room. He felt as if he was choking, as if there was some invisible force wound tight about his neck. As if by instinct, he looked down at his distorted reflection in the waxed floor. Bryden hoped in breaking his gaze with the prisoner that he might release the feeling of iron clamps about his rib cage.

To his surprise, this seemed to work.

Released, Bryden darted his gaze all about him, seeking the source for what had just happened to his. His breath returned to him by way of taking in ragged gasps of air. A roaring that had filled his ears now diminished. Bryden knew he was back to reality and once more fully aware of his surroundings. He came to the realization that not just the silent and motionless man was studying him intently, but several additional inmates had awakened and now looked at him through their bars, apparently to view the freakish event he had undergone.

The majority of them now turned and went back to their bunks, all except the sentinel. He gaze never wavered, even as Bryden stepped close to the cell front. Bryden experienced a growing rage, coupled with fear. His shadow loomed over the eerie and stoic prisoner. What Bryden saw next gave him pause.

Looking past the small man with the dark eyes, he saw cardboard inside the cell. There were the exact same kind of cardboard boxes that he had rained down hell upon just scant hours ago. The man had several handmade cat toys on his low metal table.

Bryden noticed something else. He could also see the snow falling outside, through the narrow window of the inmate's cell. The view overlooked Four Stand and P.I.

For the first time, Bryden did not feel so strong. He turned about and moved back down the hallway to the office.

There is no way in hell he saw anything, is there? he wondered. Knowing how thick the fog had been, he rationally felt this had to be the case. Yet, those dark eyes of the inmate seemed to hide something there, as if there was some dire knowledge residing inside of them.

Bryden went back to the office. He fished around for a few seconds and then retrieved the time-dulled, silver key ring from inside his pants pocket. He found the appropriate key and then pushed this in with ease. He twisted the key until he heard the tumbler make its dead "thunk" sound. Once inside, Bryden sat down hard into the chair behind the desk.

Bryden placed a cool soda can on his forehead. He felt out of sorts and needed to rest his eyes for a moment. He still felt a little odd after the incident.

He had almost dozed off when the walk officer startled him, by jokingly saying, "Okay, Bryden. Go sleep it off somewhere else, pal."

Bryden stood up and stretched his arms above his head to help wake up. He then walked toward the door.

Shift change had come and there had been a minimum of morning shift call offs. The snow blew past him in vast heaps as he left the cell-house and made his way. Again, he felt a strong presence very near him. Being in Six Cell House, he was one of the last relieved from his post. So Bryden walked the hill alone.

He could not verbalize his feelings. Not even to himself. He felt somehow accompanied by an unseen force or entity. He could see nothing beyond the wall of snow. Even so, he felt there was something there. Something setting off that part of his "animal brain" that instinctively feared. This sort of thing was new to him. This time, Bryden was the one that felt threatened and bullied by the unseen force.

Bryden could make out in the distance the flickering security light of the yard door. He would have felt a sense of relief; if not for the accompanying presence of something he feared might be spectral in nature. He hurried down the icy yard steps. He fell once, and hard enough to rattle his skull. He pulled himself up and again rushed on his way. He had to get out of there. Reaching the building, he pushed on the door.

"Open this frigging door up," he yelled.

The buzz-pop unlocking noise came, freeing up the latch. Bryden stepped through the inner gate of the Administration Building. He tasted fresh blood on his tongue, an injury from his fall, no doubt. He spat the red-tinged spittle out into the corner of the locked gate. He could hear sharp tapping sounds at the yard door. The taps joined with low but building growls.

The new control center officer was scanning in some gear. This meant he had to use a handheld tag-reader on every bit of equipment that went out onto the yard.

Now, he scanned in handcuffs left in the narrow equipment slot by the last shift's officers.

Bryden was anxious. A chorus of raspy moans and hisses were, little by little, replacing the tapping noise. Now Bryden shook the gate hard and leaned on the inner buzzer again. He eyed the yard door over his shoulder.

"This is not happening," he groaned.

The door bounced about on its frame. Bryden watched, horrified, as a dark mist closed in with intent around the outer yard window. Dark misty "hooks" of fog wormed there way in above the doorframe. He almost didn't hear the click of the middle gate opening, as he once again pushed against the gate. He tumbled down again, but this time he caught himself enough to break his fall, so he just took a half knee.

The control center officer buzzed him past the last middle gate. Bryden rushed toward the glass font wall of the control center with his equipment in hand.

The officer bent down to the slot and said, "That sounds like one hell of a storm brewing out there."

Bryden said nothing. Instead, he tossed his yard keys into the corner of the intake box and limped on to the front gate. The officer took the keys, and read the number off the chit tag attached to them. He opened the front gate.

The new officer paused, then asked as a seeming afterthought, "Okay, ain't I supposed to have signed you out with your I.D. or something?"

Bryden heard none of this. The question was lost beneath the barrage of sound reverberating from the yard door, not to mention the loud thundering hammering of his heart in his chest. Bryden just waved the man on to open the front gate.

All the time, he wondered, *How can that man not hear this noise?*

The officer's look was an exasperated expression. However, he opened the gate.

Bryden glanced back one last time. The hall beyond the yard door was now filling with the snaking black tendrils of "something." The climbing vines, as Bryden thought of them, left a dusky trail of soot along the wall. Those smoky, transparent tendrils moved forward, as they twisted and seemed to grab at the very air around them.

"Was this the monstrosity I felt?" he asked himself. Was this what had haunted his night and dogged his steps since the event happened? He felt the sick rising up and then catching in his throat. Bryden clamped his hand down hard over his mouth, preventing a shriek from spilling out. He could feel unfamiliar warmth invade his groin as he pissed himself.

"This can't be real. It can't," Bryden whispered to himself. He backed up to the door and froze there. His back pressed tight against the twin glass entrance doors. He stopped his useless mantra. He closed his eyes like a kid, wishing away a scary monster from his closet. Opening his eyes, he saw the shadows had gone. He now watched blood running dark and thick on the floor, pooling below the steps to the outside yard.

Bryden turned away and began his escape out the front double doors. He hurried down the snow-laden front steps, as he held fast to the railing to help keep him upright. He tried his best to shield his eyes with his one free hand from the prying icy daggers of snow. Bryden refused to look back this time. He was prey, and he had long experience of how prey behaved. Prey flees. It does not fight.

"Pick your battles, son," That was his motto. This was so true now, more than ever.

He became aware that the screams he'd been hearing had died away. All he heard around him now was the soft whisper of falling snow on ice. His heart still hammered hard in his chest. Bryden made his way down the last set of steps and toward his blue Ford truck.

Bryden popped the lock. He slid inside the truck and fired the engine up on the first attempt. He set the wipers and the defroster to work on clearing the windows of both snow and frozen fog.

His fear was now somewhat under control. He still wanted to waste no time in getting free of the place, though. As soon as the windshield was clear enough, he backed out. As it was late at night, he had the road to himself. The headlights reflected back, the road glowing with the falling ice. Bryden was looking forward to getting home. He had never seen anything like what he had seen this night before. Gone was the bravado of earlier. He was now a scared man.

Bryden turned onto Kentucky Highway 293, intent on heading home. He reached down to turn on the radio. He had his eyes off the road only for a second while he searched for a soothing station. The truck's wheels hit a patch of black ice. The vehicle zigzagged, fishtailing out of control, and then ran off the road. The truck crashed into a dense patch of woods.

Bryden tried his best to regain some control of the runaway vehicle. He managed to miss a couple of large stones jutting up from the earth, as if two giant spearheads trying to bar his way. The front bumper gouged huge chunks of earth out of the ground. This covered the window with a wall of fresh mud. He slammed the nose of the large Ford into a huge maple about forty-five feet down a ravine.

He had cracked his head hard against the steering wheel. The front windshield now held a spider web pattern. He could see steam coming from beneath the dash. The smell in the air was sweet. He detected the presence of leaking antifreeze. Bryden sat for a moment, stunned, and staring at the now crumpled dashboard. His eyesight had faded to near tunnel vision.

He could taste a surge of fresh blood in his mouth. He also found it was difficult to breathe through his nose. He guessed, going by the high pitch whine his nostrils made as he breathed, that his nose must be broken. He realized his truck was now wrapped around a giant tree. Moreover, he was going into shock, and did not realize this. He spit another mouthful of blood free of his swollen lips.

He began to slip into unconsciousness. Realizing this was happening, he tried to shake it off. However, like a rising tidal pool of darkness, the blackness pulled him under. He drifted off for a while, but then, at last, became conscious once more. The motor of the truck was dead. The one remaining headlight sat accrued in its mangled mount, the light dim. The dash clock told him about two hours had passed.

He knew he would have to get help, even if that meant crawling for it. However, he found he was too weak to push the door open. The now two-foot tall snowdrifts had wedged the door shut. He banged his fist against the warped dash. Then he heard movement in the back seat.

He tried to turn his head to catch a glimpse of the source of the phantom sound. He discovered what it was. The sound was emanating from the horror that had chased him out of the prison yard door. This nightmare was making that same scratching, growling noise. He was close enough to kiss the horror's gnashing teeth. The crawling hell was inside the car and the beast was hungry. It hungered for him. Bryden lost consciousness.

Morning came and a local semi-truck driver called in that he had seen a truck down in a deep ditch. The local sheriff had put out flares on the road above the drop-off. The sheriff then repelled down the hill to the battered vehicle. He had to maneuver past tangled tree limbs and the rutted earth.

The sheriff moved alongside the passenger door. He played his flashlight's beam through the frosted window of the vehicle. Seeing someone, he called for an ambulance. Then the sheriff tried to force the door open, several times before giving up. He prepared to shatter the window but then thought better of it. Using with a small crowbar, he dug the black metal bar into the seam of the door.

He fought the frozen door this way for a few tense minutes. Then he felt the lock break free. With a final defiant pull, he caused the door to yawn open. A flurry of activity occurred around him. Cats, seemingly dozens of them, poured out of the gaping doorway. The sheriff covered his head, defending his eyes from possible scratches. When the car door was clear, he flashed his light into the vehicle.

What he saw next made him gasp in repulsion. There was a man. Well, this had been a man. What he saw now was a mutilated corpse. The corpse was missing its nose, eyes, and most of the right side of his face. The truck's interior was awash in blood. The remaining remnant of the man's face was contorted, as if in a final scream. He would have had trouble doing this. In his lap was the dead man's severed tongue.

Bryden awoke, screaming. He was behind the Six Cell House's walk desk, and his motions made him fall backward into the shelf that held the riot batons. The hickory staffs tumbled down onto the floor, knocking over the wastebasket. Bryden climbed to his knees, next to the wastebasket's scattered contents. He sat there, wide-eyed and stunned, with tears streaming down his wet cheeks. He found he had vomited, so powerful had been the vision or nightmare.

Bryden cleaned up the throw-up, as well as picking up the scattered batons. He tried to compose himself before the Six Cell House officer returned. When he did, Bryden exited the cell house with caution. He was relieved to see the snow had stopped. There was six inches of fresh powder on the hill as he made his way out of the prison.

He saw no ghouls or ghostly visions. The few sounds he heard on top of the hill were the faint screams of the winds. He did not encounter any spirits looking to exact revenge on him for all his wrongdoings. The horror he had envisioned coming after him was nowhere on his path.

Climbing into his perfectly fine truck, Bryden exited the parking lot and headed home. The feeling of unease slowly left him as the distance between him and the prison grew. A growing sensation of normality returned to him. On his way, he stopped and bought a case of beer, but could only finish a six-pack. The beer he drank only served to make him queasy. The dark visions he had endured earlier that night were just too damned real to forget in one evening of drinking. No matter how he tried, he could not get the night's events out of his head. Bryden had laughed at killing those cats. He now had only regret for that.

Bryden sat up until dawn. He called into the dayshift captain and told him he wasn't feeling right and so was taking a sick day.

His memories, it seemed, were still too fresh to walk back into that prison yet. Later, Bryden went to his doctor and managed to get stress leave. This sort of leave is for staff in times of extreme emotional problems.

Those dark tendrils groping toward him haunted his dreams. He would catch glimpses of small shadows throughout the day. Doors opened and shut seemingly of their own accord. This paranormal activity to the human mind is taxing. The damage for Bryden was lasting.

He would not be able to return to the prison, Bryden knew that now. Whenever he attempted to approach the prison, he had bouts of sickness and heard the screams of hundreds of cats. Bryden felt the oppression would continue if he returned to work at the penitentiary. He used up the remainder of his sick time to find another job. He had his uniforms returned by a friend, citing health issues as his reason for not returning them himself.

However, the night terrors and the oppression of the shadows continued. Bryden debated on having a preacher come bless the house. However, intrinsically, he knew it wasn't the house that had ghosts. He was the one haunted by, terrorized by the slinking dark figures.

The dreams and shadows became so bad that one night he called out to the entity he felt was doing all of this. He screamed, "I'm sorry for the killing and the abuse. I can't take this any longer. I'll never touch another cat or any animal ever again. Please, just forgive me. Please just make this stop."

Bryden then rose and walked, as if commanded against his will to do so, to his closet. He reached inside and picked up his boots. Those same boots that had once been covered in streaks of blood from the night this nightmare had started. He stood there, trembling for a moment. This, for him, was very much like handling a murder weapon now. Bryden left the house by way of his back door and headed to a barrel he used for burning trash.

He tossed the boots into the barrel and lit them on fire. Bryden felt he had no say in this, for the force was in command. The boots hissed as they began to melt. An eerie, blue-green flame rose from them, and again Bryden shook. He dropped to his knees beside the flaming barrel and taking in a great gasp of air. Whatever force had him in its grip, now released him.

He looked ahead at the ground. All of the small shadows left his side and disappeared in midair as they glided toward the edge of his yard. The oppression that held him suddenly left. Bryden, at last, felt forgiven.

The account of this tale says that he then moved out west. He settled near Las Vegas, somewhere close to the high deserts where there are few cats to find. This lesson came at a high price for him. After hearing this tale, I knew that I would never look at a prison cat in quite the same way again and always, I gave them the respect they deserved.

CHAPTER 17

THE BLACK SHELF

Many paranormal events seem to happen on cold, rainy nights. Many experts agree the storms might provide energy for spirits to manifest. This story takes place in one of the protective custody units. This is on the fourth floor of Five Cell House. Protective custody, or PC, is meant for fragile or at-risk inmates. This is a relatively new practice. Too many weaker inmates often were found dead in their cells, so I guess they decided to separate them from the general population, or GP inmates. They wear green, colored-coded uniforms. Most at KSP call them leprechauns because of this.

An officer told this story to me. Let us call him Ed. He was the walk officer on the fourth floor that night. Ed recounted to me that there was an institutional review coming up that week. They had the inmate painters repainting everything. In true Kentucky Department of Corrections style, this was all last minute. All day, they swarmed like ants over the cell houses. This was one of the many reasons Ed liked morning shift. There was less "brass" and inmates stayed in their cells.

The time was just after 3:00 a.m. This had been a rainy day, and thunder was rumbling to signal that his shift was going to be a waterlogged night, as well. The cell house had the unique cologne odor of feet and body odor. This was accented with just a hint of paint fumes and tobacco smoke.

Ed had been busy finishing paperwork. This was the glamour of state work. The workload is ninety percent paperwork. The job is less law enforcement and more office worker. This was fine with Ed. He had been there just short of ten years. He liked the repetitiveness of it all, the reliability of it.

Ed had to be careful not to touch the walls surrounding the painted office shelf. The paint was still wet. The walls were a uniform and functional, battleship gray. The shelf was almost gaudy by contrast. It had been painted black rather than gray.

His watch beeped 4:00 a.m. Ed updated his security logbook, while the storm came at full force outside. The rain pummeled the narrow office window behind his small desk. It appeared is if it was raining sideways, so hard did it come down. Ed said that one could not see a thing out of the security window, except for the flares of light of the lightning strikes, which were followed by the bone-jarring peals of thunder. The power went out every half hour or so. The generators would kick on if the grid became overwhelmed in this way. Most things in KSP were old and the power grid was no different in this respect.

Ed hurried through his round on the walks. The combination of flickering power and inmates in the dark gave him the motivation to speed on through this task. He made note of the hall windows leaking onto the floor.

Christ, this place is like a frigging sinking ship! he thought. He was more than ready to end the lousy night. On his last walk, the lights went out and stayed out. The Maglite was all but broken. The flashlight only cast a dim, weak beam. The light illuminated the hall just well enough to get back to the office. Ed managed to unlock the office.

He stumbled into the tiny cubbyhole of a place and groped for the light switch. The power was still out. His was a modern and conditioned response to darkness. Flip the switch and fill a room with light. Dispel the demons hiding in the inky shadows. Only, in this case, it hadn't worked.

He managed to slide the Maglite into the cradle on the wall and then plopped down into his office chair. He sat there sipping his now cold and stale coffee. Chatter squawked on his walkie-talkie. The engineers had arrived to try to get the generators up and going.

He wondered how long this would take and if the power would be on by let-out. The time was close to six. The rain had at last died down. There was still the occasional streak of phosphorus-like illumination from the lightning flashes. The night was quiet now, other than for the sound of drips from the pooling rain on the roof. The rain had produced a thick fog that covered the hillside and topped the barbed wire that danced in the wind along the top of the prison wall. The dense fog clung to the landscape and smothered any possible glimmers of pre-morning light.

Ed sat there, feeling odd. He was not sure why, and he did not like this sensation. He finished his security log. Now, he had the distinct feeling of some sort of a presence. He knew no one was out of the cells, and no one had come onto the walk. He would have heard the gate unlock if so. He, along with his dilapidated Maglite, ran one last round. The flashlight worked well up until he approached the office. The flashlight's beam dimmed and faded out at that point.

There is something very telling in fear. Ed's hands gripped the Maglite like a drowning man might cling to some rescuer. His pulse throbbed in his temples. He managed to sit in his seat in the darkened office. He needed to calm himself, control his breathing. The puzzling thing was he wasn't at all sure why he felt that way to begin with.

The lights repeatedly flashed on and off. The storm had apparently blown out a lot more hardware and so caused a cascade of power failures. He signed off on the logbook. Ed knew his relief officer would be there before long. The fog had been pulling back. A light drizzle had pushed the dense mist away. One could now just about make out the gothic peaks of the prison wall. He had just enough pale light to maneuver without banging his legs on the heavy old desk. Ed decided to put his mind to other tasks.

He cleaned off his desk. He was leaning over, wiping up the watered-down prison cleaning spray. Something passed between the pale light, and what he was doing. The air moved, causing a chill to run right up his back.

Something drew his attention to the shelf. He leveled his eyes on the shimmering, onyx-toned shelf. Ed saw the reflection of an amorphous blob. This was a shadowy thing and it appeared only semi-solid.

"No, this is just a product of the conditions here tonight, a delusion. I refuse to validate this with fear," he commanded himself. He rubbed his eyes like a child intent on wiping away a monster from the corner of a bedroom. He hesitantly opened his eyes. What he saw next curdled his blood, for the thing was now in the shape of a man.

There was even a face, one twisted by hate and evil intent. He was dressed in inmate 1920s garb. The thing raised its hands. They looked like long, clawed grabbing hooks, seemingly meant to strangle him.

Ed had a choice to make: fight or flight. He snapped up the nearby flashlight and pushed away from his desk. He kicked the seat back against the wall where the spectral horror was.

Ed spun around and leveled the Maglite straight at the man's head. The battered flashlight's beam passed through the thing's head as if he was made of vapor. Ed stared dumbfounded.

"Jesus Christ! What are you?" Ed bellowed. Stumbling back, fists clenched, he wondered how one went about fighting smoke?

Then, the lights bust into life. Ed never even noticed, so intent was he on this nemesis. The man-like creature began to fade. The ghost dissolved then, as if it had never been. Ed retrieved his keys and coat, locked the office, and sprinted outside the main, four-walk gate.

He was halfway down the stairway when he heard the bottom, Five Cell House door unlocked. What a wonderful sound that was for him.

After handing the keys in to his relief, he went to the office and turned in his badge. Ed had seen enough. He gave no explanation to them, beyond saying, "You can't pay me enough to come back there again."

After that, Ed was a changed man. He left corrections forever. Some experiences one has lived through, it seems, can haunt a person from then on. If one was to go in that dark gray office today, you could still see that shiny black shelf there as if waiting. The ghost could well be waiting also. If so, it waits for another stormy night, and the right soul to appear to and then torment.

CHAPTER 18

THE GIRL THAT CRIED GHOST

A KSP Supervisor related the following event to me. This is a perfect example of the fact that not everyone is able to brave those bumps in the night that resound deep inside the old prison gates.

I had contacted my friend. Let us call him, "T." He and I had been taking about our old days together at the prison, and of course, felt obliged to recount "war stories" from our time there. He knew I had investigated many haunted locations, and our discussion turned to all the odd things I had seen there at the prison.

I should mention at this point that T was no lightweight. A solid 6'2", and a low-key type of guy, he certainly was, but God help anyone if they were an inmate trying to hurt any of his officers. T was a dependable man, one that could be counted upon. Moreover, he was not prone to flights of fancy and tall tales.

I asked T, "So what is the weirdest or scariest thing you have ever seen, heard, or dealt with at the prison?"

He gave an introspective pause. Then he replied in a flat tone of voice, "I have felt some odd things, heard some stuff, too. But the oddest thing was what happened to this one girl some years back. It was before you came to work there."

Okay, now I was intrigued. I had never heard this. He had me hooked.

"Well, man," I said. "You must tell me. Just what did happen?"

T continued by saying, "The event was in either 2001 or 2002, but I can't remember which. Still, this was the craziest thing I ever saw firsthand."

T said he had been working in Three Cell House all the time back then. That night, he was working as a yard officer. He had been doing his yard security check. This included checking locks, fences, and fire and safety gear. Not having those essential emergency items ready could lead to many people being injured, or even to their deaths, in the event of an emergency. His shift captain radioed him. He needed T to come to Four Cell House.

This sort of command happens a lot when a female is working in the Four Cell House control center. The small bathroom they had there was an empty cell on the walk, and most refused to use it. I cannot say I blame them, either. Sitting scant feet from murderers and rapists does not help one to urinate without restraint.

The ten-wall stand officer hit the button that controlled the kitchen and Four Cell House yard gate With the locks released, T made his way down the steps to Four Cell House outside gate. Understand that inmate movement is strictly controlled at KSP, and everywhere there are stairs. "They were knee-crushers, the man-hobblers," T used to call them. He took them slow. A big man falling down those steep stone stairs would be in for a bad time.

He hit the gate buzzer; the wind was up that night and he looked forward to getting inside, and out of the cool weather. He then buzzed the inside door button and stepped inside.

The walk officer was not at his desk. T walked to the windows of Four Cell House control. He wanted to know where the man was.

The woman working there said, "He's at the Twenty River Walk shower. Are you my relief?"

He replied in the affirmative. Then he noticed the expression on her face. She looked like someone had just walked over her grave. Her eyes were gigantic, and she wore a frantic look. She also shifted from foot to foot, as if in extreme agitation.

Noting this, T then walked across the cell house floor, toward the stairs that led down to Twenty Walk. He had seen the apprehension in her eyes, and now couldn't get the sight out of his mind.

"What hell is going on in here?" he asked himself. He descended the stairs, passing the mop room and the pipe chases to the cell house. Farther along, he saw the walk officer flashing his light about. The officer was a "fish." This is an old inmate term for a fresh-to-the-system inmate or guard.

T could hear the inmates complaining. One asked him, "Captain T, Captain' T, man, you got to get that fish to stop flashing lights all night. I'm not sure what he's looking for, but if he ain't found it yet, he ain't going to."

T told the old convict he would take care of things. T then walked the new officer back up to his desk, telling him to douse the light.

"What's going on, officer?" he asked.

The officer replied, "Sir, I don't know. I was making a round when the control officer hailed me on the walkie-talkie, half-sobbing to get down to the shower area right away. She refuses to say what she's seen or heard to me. Is she cracking up or what, man?"

T replied, "Hey now, that's a fellow officer and a woman, so show some respect. It is odd, though."

By this time, she was back on the radio with T, begging to be relieved. She was ready to tear a hole in the wall, if necessary. She seemed almost frantic. Upon their return, she buzzed him into the gates into Four Cell House control. Then she met him at the door, wanting to leave right away.

T sat her down. He wanted to try to get some clue as to what had scared this woman half out of her mind. T knew her to be a good officer. She was a logical person, he knew, so to see her in this condition was troubling.

"All right, just what in the hell is up? This doesn't seem like a piss break; what's really going on?" T asked.

She laughed as if he would never believe it. She said, "Okay, I'll tell you, and then, can you please get me the hell out of here?"

T fought back a chuckle. This was not meant in a cruel or judgmental way, but he felt it was such an odd way to be asked.

"Ten-four," he assured her.

She explained she had been cleaning the switchboards that control the inmate movement in and out of cells, and into the cell house. Then, suddenly, she started feeling weird, as if something was watching her.

She continued, "I updated my log book, when something compelled me on, causing me to look up at the walk cameras. There was a weird kind of movement, not quite a shadow, yet a little more solid looking. The dark form ran along the cell fronts, then sank into the walk floor...

"I assumed at first that it was a bug or a cobweb, something ordinary. But it just wasn't." She began to tremble again at this point and started to chew on her nails. T gave her a second to get herself in control.

"Right, you are almost done," he said. "After this, you can go take a break, go do whatever you need to do." T said to her as added encouragement.

She had taken another long draw on her cigarette. She expelled the vaporous mist from her lungs and then sighed.

She said, "Great T, fine, I'll tell you what I saw after that. Then, I'm out of here," she added, seeming as much to herself, as to T. "I looked away, not sure what I saw. I've worked here a time or two before, but never had any real issues until now. Nothing like tonight," she added. She moved in closer then and locked eyes with T. It seemed she meant to make sure there was no room for miscommunication about what she had to say next.

She said, "I pulled myself together, saying this was a trick of the light, or smoke, or anything but what the oddity really was. However, it started again.

"The thing appeared more solid now. The entity knew I saw it, and I think it was somehow feeding on my fear."

"Then what happened?" T asked. "What else did you experience there?" He was now feeling some of the excitement and had a touch more understanding of why this had her so scared.

"The shape rolled and morphed, moving up through the shower stalls from one shower head to another," she said, between taking short breaths. The strain on her was now obvious to T.

"The thing somehow became a head with a pale sort of face." She began a non-stop sobbing at this point. Huddled now like a frightened child, she just kept saying over and over, "The horrible thing was a head, a grinning skull, just floating there with long yellowed teeth."

T sat there, slack-jawed. He was not sure, in truth, what to say to aid the young woman. He had no idea what she had really seen, but whatever it had been, it was something that had reduced her to a sobbing mess.

After a few minutes to give her a chance to collect herself, he had her escorted out of Four Cell House. After seeing the shift captain, she left the institution.

She had to have someone come to drive her home, due to her condition. She never came back to Four Cell House or to The Kentucky State Penitentiary again. She tendered her resignation the next morning by phone. Some thought that maybe she was just trying to get out of work, others that she had been on drugs or was emotionally or mentally unstable.

T told me, "To this day, Asher, I still can't say for sure. My rational mind says this must be something else. However, the look in her eyes... it still haunts me." Law enforcement is, mostly, a world of black and white, of absolutes. However, sometimes, things play havoc on the safety of conformity and order. Sometimes, the darkness demands an audience, despite manmade, or perhaps even natural, laws.

CHAPTER 19

THE DANCING SKULL

"The prison is a greedy, torturous machine. It's one that grinds strong men raw and drives weak men mad." This was the quote given to me by one retired officer. He had worked at the Kentucky State Penitentiary and so I felt sure he knew what he was talking about consider the nature of that place.

A real old-timer told me this next paranormal occurrence. For the sake of anonymity, again, I will not use his real name. Let us just call him Lou. I had the chance to interview Lou after some time had passed since his time as a public servant. Fifty years had passed since the occurrence he had endured. I met with Lou at his austere home in Princeton, Kentucky.

He was a rather unassuming looking person. Lou looked much like any man in his late eighties. He had a weathered, somewhat round, face and a crew cut. He had wisps of whitish red hair for eyebrows. Lou was the product of simple working folk, yet there was something more to him. There was something unsettling in his eyes. They seemed to hold you. They were the eyes of a man that had seen war and death, and it showed.

Lou at first spoke of generalities, like food strikes and the everyday duties that conscripted a man to dole out his time in segments of chores, and not days. Even though I had misgivings about this, I pressed him more. I began to ask about the paranormal. He at first seemed more than happy to avoid these subjects.

"Can you tell me about that night in the early 1960s? Can you tell about the night that the incident occurred?" I asked.

I stood and watched Lou for a moment. He seemed like a man out of time. He exhaled for a moment. He tried to push the recollection to a safe distance in his mind, I could see. He walked across the faded, beige shag carpet of the living room and sat down on the worn, high-backed chair there.

Lou reached into the small dresser next to the chair and pulled out two glasses of Kentucky sipping whiskey. Filling them both, he offered me a glass. There is a Kentucky tradition that, before any memorable act, there is a need to share a small glass of spirits. This was true of either somber or joyous events. We both had taken a sip. We then took the time to savor the distinctive flavors. Beyond the soft clink of our glasses as we placed them down was the faint whistle of a distant train.

Lou rubbed his grey beard with his free hand. He broke the silence by saying, "Well I guess we should talk a little. What do you know about KSP?"

I recounted to him my years in corrections, and touched on some of the things I had seen and experienced.

Lou, nodding his head, replied, "Hmm. You might not think I'm crazy, once I tell you this, after all."

I assured him I held no doubt to the keenness of his faculties. This seemed to ease his apprehension a bit.

"KSP was a different animal back then, son," Lou said. "This was a time of civil unrest. There wasn't anywhere that was as lethal as old Maggie's."

He told me this had all happened on a weekend shift.

"On duty that day was the skeleton crew. This is what they called my old crew that ran the prison," Lou said. He took another strong sip of his whiskey.

"I was just a kid." He leveled his eyes at me. "Understand this, I've never told this to anyone outside the prison. Not even my wife knew."

I reassured him that I would keep his name out of the story, and that I empathized with him. I said, "I can't imagine carrying this alone for fifty years."

Lou's demeanor softened a bit, as he replied, "Thank you, thank you for understanding this."

I was nervous, so I shifted on my heels. I tried to smile if only to reassure him, but the smile felt fake. He was presenting this dark gift to me. I had to treat this with trust with respect. The events he spoke of still haunt me.

The story is as follows and is in his words. I rely on his portrayal of the facts as presented here.

"I had got there just after the afternoon count," he said, by way of a start. "This was in mid-August. The temperature was hotter than hell out there on top of the prison yard. The yard was like an oven then. There wasn't a soul out there on that hill. The day's temperature was pushing well over 100 degrees by then.

"Whenever inclement weather hits the prison, the inmates lay low. Convicts are survivors. They had to gain life skills on the hill or die. I had just reported to the yard office, to find out what my day's assignment were to be. There had been a lot of tension between the guards and inmates due to mistreatment at the time.

"I did not say *alleged* mistreatment. Those things actually happened. Some people would say they were just 'rules that were in play for a different time.' This is a true statement. Although right is right. I was not an 'inmate lover' or an advocate. Still, I could not deny the conditions those men survived were brutal. The shift captains expected swift and immediate response to anyone seeming to be ducking the rules.

"We had moved away from public floggings by then, at least. We did turn the screws on the inmates in other ways, though.

Locking down the yard was a major deterrent. Cutting the rations in the inmate kitchen also helped. There was also suspending the visits they received from family, and turning off the water to the cell houses."

The prison still works like this to a surprising extent. The inmates know that we will get the institution back after a riot, one way or another. An uprising comes along fast and without warning. This was the same sad song that has been played at KSP for over one hundred years. At the time of Lou's event, the penitentiary was even more volatile than it is now. The inmates on the yard were tense and in high alert. They had even less to lose by acting up than inmates of today, because they had less to begin with.

"There had been a series of stabbings and rapes over the first quarter of the year. The shot-caller among the convicts of the time was William Raines, a.k.a. the 'Worm,' who instigated the attacks. Raines had just gotten out of a stay in segregation and was looking for payback. Losing face in any situation is not good for someone like him. Inside of Kentucky's most dangerous prison, this became a life or death scenario.

"The yard was now open for the inmates to use. They were not to go near the fences by Three Cell House, where they had the back door opened up. The hoses ended a disturbance in one of the lower cells and now they had the janitors pushing the excess water out through the walk. I've seen the water pick up full-grown men and slam them into the bars.

"Anyway, Raines gained the nickname Worm due to the worm-looking, snake tattoo on his right hand. He had been quiet since getting out of the hole. Solitary time plays hell with a man's mind. Everyone assumed he was still a bit rattled and so not much of a threat. That whole day went much as any other. Still, I just wasn't able to shake an odd feeling. My gut twisted up over something and so I left the top of that hill fast.

"Shift change came and after a bit of last-minute paperwork, I was out of there. I was in my truck and a good mile down the curvy road before that strange turning in my stomach subsided. I turned left off that road toward old highway 293. I saw a nightshift officer ripping around that curve just then. He looked late and pissed off.

"I gave him a casual wave. He tore past me, kicking up dust and gravel in the process. He never batted an eye.

"*What a horse's ass*, I had thought to myself, as I watched his lights disappear around another curve. I contented myself with some Hank Williams Sr. on the radio. I was thinking about just getting home and not much else.

"My missus had already gone to bed by the time I got home. I kicked off my shoes outside and opened the screened-in door. I ate the beef roast she had left me in the oven and settled in for the night. I got into bed and did my best not to rouse her. I had a headache and was thankful to be able to go straight to bed. I began to drift off into sleep.

"*What had been the matter with me at work today?* I wondered to myself. Then I forgot about it. I rolled over and was away in a dream in minutes.

"In the darkness, I heard the sound of feet and bellowing and there was the smell of smoke. I looked around me, bewildered that I was on the hill. How was this possible? The prison was a madhouse. You could see figures darting about in the shadows. They moved just beyond a fire.

"My skin tightened from the heat. I found myself half-running, half-crawling on hands and knees to find shelter from the chaos. I found a low concrete wall by the infirmary, the sounds of shattering glass and cries of terror and yells of excitement all mingled together. This, coupled with the rolling black smoke billowing up across the yard, guaranteed to make things unclear as to just who were friend or foe.

"I coughed from the foul smoke that threatened to choke me. I did my best to stop this before I had a full-on coughing fit. There was movement all around me. I kept my hands balled-up to defend myself. I waited for any chance to find a way to make a break and run for help.

"I could hear the sound of the sally port gate. Loud bangs rose from that direction. I was unsure if the sound was inmates or officers. I heard the last of the clamoring start to move farther away from where I hid. The one thought in my mind was survive this.

"The combination of sweat and smoke stung my eyes. The sharp gravel bit into my knees like needles.

"'How can this be possible? I was in bed just a minute ago,' I whispered to myself. My mind raced about in search on what to do. I had to get some idea of what was out in front of me. I felt in my pocket for my Zippo and I found the shiny case. I slowly lifted the lighter up above my blind.

"The area out in front appeared clearer now. I knew I had to find a safer spot. I pulled up to a crouched position. I moved in a low run. I ran past several men, out and away from my small hiding spot. Every convict was looking to escape. I saw before me a flaming battlefield. I heard several screams out in the thick walls of smoke. As I edged up toward the yard officer, I heard movement nearby.

"I pulled in tight against the side of the building. To my right, I could hear footsteps coming up the concrete steps leading up from the prison-walking track to the yard office front door. From the outlines of the ghost-like forms, I figured that they were the same men I had just passed. They seemed to have realized I was a guard and this was a good time to get in on the fun.

"I had no radio or any sort of weapon to fend off a mob of amp-up ghostly inmates. They stopped near me. They appeared to be talking about which way I may have gone. I crept further down toward to left of the front of the building. Two of the lurking figures were fading into the smoke had gone off up the hill searching for me there. The other four turned my way.

"I was in a panic. The wind had started to shift and they might see me in seconds. Lunging into a full run, I rounded the left side of the brick building. I hit a thick wall of smoke from one of the burning buildings. I had managed to keep on my feet despite the smoking debris and broken glass. I ran toward the sally port gate. I felt a searing pain gouge into my right thigh. Losing my footing, I tumbled and slid on my face and shoulders against the surface of the rocky access road and then into the security fence.

"My vision filled with dirt, blood, and smoke. I endured a barrage of blows to my ribs, face, and back. I spat out a mouthful of blood. I managed to see a hand appear out of the thinning smoke. My consciousness dimmed. I made out another hand with a snake tattoo. This fist held a shank or homemade prison knife. As my mind sank into the darkness of unconsciousness, I felt the slicing of the blade across my exposed throat. Hot torrents of blood jetted out onto the ground below."

Lou then paused. All I could hear was the clock announcing the hour.

I said to him, "Lou, I don't understand." I had taken a large gulp of the liquor. He looked up as I did this. His face was white and blotchy, wet with old fear.

"Let me finish this, I need to finish this," he said, in a distant-sounding voice.

I looked at Lou's throat. I saw no evidence of what should be very big and very old scar from the attack there.

"I came to and I was sobbing," he said. "The blackness was gone and replaced by light streaming in through the window. My face was in my hands and I was huddled in one corner of my bedroom, trembling. My wife tried to calm me. I told her I just had a prison dream. I omitted the being murdered part. I did not want any part of that place getting to her.

"I pushed aside what I had experienced. I had to. I had breakfast and dressed for work. I felt such dread as I went through the steel gates of the prison. I went to roll call and then onto the yard. Over the radio, came an all-officer's call for assistance. I neared Six Cell House. I heard someone say, 'There's one hanging, cap,' from within the open cell house door.

"The walk officer was clearing out the inmates so medical could get to the site. I skirted the mass of people that rolled down the hall towards me. I pulled in tight and approached the grey cell front. There were officers in there, cutting the sheet the inmate was hanging from. I saw the body was Worm Raines.

"His face was twisted into a garish combination of horror and hate. I had to look away. This was the same face I'd just as I'd seen it exactly in the dark vision. I noticed he had scribbled all over his floor. 'Pay the price.' This was everywhere, over the walls, floor and the ceiling.

"This was a hardcore convict. I wondered to myself, what could force his hand to do this to himself?

"I stood watch at the cell front once the doctor got there to examine the body. A quick examination followed. The doctor declared him dead. The coroner soon came to retrieve the body. We loaded the cadaver into a vehicle and the yard supervisor and I drove to the sally port. Once the coroner arrived, we would give him the body to be disposed of per the inmate's wishes.

"As we waited, the supervisor said, 'You know, it's kind of ironic. This was no more than twenty-five feet from here where that riot happened years ago.

"'It was then I felt the sickness come to my guts again,'" he continued. 'It resulted in a shift commander having his throat slit. We didn't release this fact to the public, but they sawed off his head. They paraded his decapitated head around the yard. They left the horrid trophy in front of the yard office. This was never proven, but I know it was Worm who did it.'

"This was common to keep certain darker details of a murder quiet, out of respect of the victim's family. Nothing good comes by sharing ghoulish past incidents. I'm one of the few officers still alive that knows the true details of that night. This is on you now to carry. This is yours to do with as you wish."

Lou finished his drink. He leaned in toward me and said, "I asked to be relieved by another yard officer. I walked into the captain's office and turned in my badge. That was my last day at KSP. I couldn't walk that yard another second." His face still showed the stress of a man that has carried a great weight for a long time.

I sat there dumbfounded for a moment, and then said, "How is this possible? I mean what happened?"

Lou shook his head. "All I can tell you is that I was there and I felt this haunting. I feel that the spirit of the supervisor wanted someone to know what really happened. I still can't say why he showed his murder to me. I only hope that the man found the peace deserved by the dead."

I cannot say that we all had spiritual visitations for any specific reason. I can say that these events have connected all of us in some unspoken way; all of us who have experience them at KSP. There are things in life both strange and fascinating. The same seems to hold true for death. I have no concrete opinions about this haunting, psychic experience, or whatever it was, Lou had.

In the end, after speaking with Lou, I walked out of there more confident than ever that the things I have seen and felt were true, were real. I know from the look on his face and the tone of his voice that he believed what he saw. He felt every word that he spoke.

Paranormal researchers believe that the dead will reach out to those they feel will listen. Sometimes, all the dead require is recognition in order to be able to cross over. The spirits inside the Kentucky State Penitentiary still haunt the steps of employees. Nobody walks away unmarked or un-bloodied from their time at the prison.

CONCLUSION

What is there left to say about the Kentucky State Penitentiary and the paranormal activity there that will better explain what I know to be true? Events would seem to have to speak for themselves in this case.

The penitentiary had haunted me for many years before I ever stepped inside the heavy metal gates. The prison has been many things to me in my life. Each aspect carries different emotions with it.

The penitentiary was a cautionary tale as a child.

"Don't not screw up, or you might end up inside of their fence, breaking rocks," was what my father often told me. He knew this better than most. His father served time at the Kentucky State Penitentiary when my father was but a wee boy. This event colored his mindset and motivated him to pursue a life as a police officer. The prison had marked him whether he liked it or not, just as it had marked his father before him.

The penitentiary then became a source of gainful employment for me as a young adult. The state implemented an adoption credit. We were able to use this to adopt two special little boys into our family. Working as a correctional officer helped feed and house my family for over ten years. I learned many things in my years of employment there. I did hear a large number of people's experiences and had several of my own, as well, as this book illustrates.

I've been able to take those experiences as an author and use them as the subject of this book. Writing this was quite an adventure in and of itself. The hunt to track down everyone I had spoken about in the book was a daunting process. They ranged everywhere from former co-workers, and local acquaintances, to inmates who have gone on to productive lives after having served their time at the castle.

I connect these experiences with my own and I can say without any doubt that I believe the Kentucky State Penitentiary is haunted. Based on my long history as a paranormal investigator, along with my firsthand experiences, I know that the testimonies of numerous people cannot all be fantasy. Their conviction with regard to what they have told me only goes to magnify my beliefs in this regard. In any case, what else would one expect from the most notorious institution in Kentucky? If hauntings exist, then surely this place is haunted.

I wanted to present this all to the reader in a way that was factual and yet still entertaining. I wanted to make everyone keep that light on, so to speak. If I can bring the real-life paranormal accounts of the prison to the curious public, I will have met my goal. The kid in me hopes you all get a good fright out of them, too.

The writing of this book had stirred many emotions and memories in me. They are both good and painful. This book was cathartic in a way for me. I had carried these accounts of KSP's strange paranormal phenomenon with me for many years. I now pass them onto the reader. This frees me of the responsibility I had felt as their guardian. I may yet again walk those halls someday, when the prison has become a museum. For now, I am content to keep the history alive and to tell the tale, and to stay well away from that penitentiary, as long as it remains one.

ACKNOWLEDGMENTS

Permuted Press

Rob Shelsky thank you for finding and fanning the writer's light within me. You are more than my mentor, you are my friend.

Michael L.Wilson and Hannah Yancey thank you for giving the means to publish my work.

Mathew Baugh and Bobbie Metevier thank you for polishing this book to a high sheen.

Lastly, I'd like to thank those connected to the prison who entrusted me with their encounters.

ABOUT THE AUTHOR

Paranormal researcher Steve E. Asher is also a freelance writer and artist, as well as a lover of music. Previously he worked over ten years in law enforcement and as a correctional officer.

Steve is a longtime researcher of the paranormal. He has traveled worldwide, most recently to Thailand where he and his wife adopted one of their two sons. Steve is an avid lover of the nighttime. He has said this is when he feels most truly alive, in the darkness of the night, and therefore most productive in his paranormal research and writing. He is a native of Princeton Kentucky.

PERMUTED PRESS
needs **you** to help

SPREAD (THE) INFECTION

FOLLOW US!

f | Facebook.com/PermutedPress
🐦 | Twitter.com/PermutedPress

REVIEW US!

Wherever you buy our book, they can be reviewed! We want to know what you like!

GET INFECTED!

Sign up for our mailing list at
PermutedPress.com

PERMUTED
PRESS

14

Peter Clines

Padlocked doors.
Strange light fixtures. Mutant
cockroaches.

There are some odd things about
Nate's new apartment. Every
room in this old brownstone has
a mystery. Mysteries that stretch
back over a hundred years.
Some of them are in plain sight.
Some are behind locked doors.
And all together these mysteries
could mean the end of Nate and
his friends.

Or the end of everything...

PERMUTED
PRESS

THE JOURNAL SERIES
by Deborah D. Moore

After a major crisis rocks the nation, all supply lines are shut down. In the remote Upper Peninsula of Michigan, the small town of Moose Creek and its residents are devastated when they lose power in the middle of a brutal winter, and must struggle alone with one calamity after another.

The Journal series takes the reader head first into the fury that only Mother Nature can dish out. Book Five coming soon!

PERMUTED
PRESS

Michael Clary
THE GUARDIAN | THE REGULATORS | BROKEN

When the dead rise up and take over the city, the Government is forced to close off the borders and abandon the remaining survivors. Fortunately for them, a hero is about to be chosen...a Guardian that will rise up from the ashes to fight against the dead. The series continues with Book Four: *Scratch*.

Emily Goodwin
CONTAGIOUS | DEATHLY CONTAGIOUS

During the Second Great Depression, twenty-four-year-old Orissa Penwell is forced to drop out of college when she is no longer able to pay for classes. Down on her luck, Orissa doesn't think she can sink any lower. She couldn't be more wrong. A virus breaks out across the country, leaving those that are infected crazed, aggressive and very hungry.

The saga continues in Book Three: *Contagious Chaos* and Book Four: *The Truth is Contagious*.

PERMUTED
PRESS

THE BREADWINNER | Stevie Kopas

The end of the world is not glamorous. In a matter of days the human race was reduced to nothing more than vicious, flesh hungry creatures. There are no heroes here. Only survivors. The trilogy continues with Book Two: *Haven* and Book Three: *All Good Things*.

THE BECOMING | Jessica Meigs

As society rapidly crumbles under the hordes of infected, three people—Ethan Bennett, a Memphis police officer; Cade Alton, his best friend and former IDF sharpshooter; and Brandt Evans, a lieutenant in the US Marines—band together against the oncoming crush of death and terror sweeping across the world. The story continues with Book Two: *Ground Zero*.

THE INFECTION WAR | Craig DiLouie

As the undead awake, a small group of survivors must accept a dangerous mission into the very heart of infection. This edition features two books: *The Infection* and *The Killing Floor*.

OBJECTS OF WRATH | Sean T. Smith

The border between good and evil has always been bloody... Is humanity doomed? After the bombs rain down, the entire world is an open wound; it is in those bleeding years that William Fox becomes a man. After The Fall, nothing is certain. *Objects of Wrath* is the first book in a saga spanning four generations.

PERMUTED
PRESS

PERMUTED
PRESS

A PREPPER'S
COOKBOOK

*20 Years of
Cooking in the
Woods*

by Deborah D. Moore

In the event of a disaster, it isn't
enough to have food. You also
have to know what to do with it.

Deborah D. Moore, author of *The
Journal* series and a passionate
Prepper for over twenty years,
gives you step-by-step instructions
on making delicious meals from
the emergency pantry.